Lippincott's

Cabinet Histories of the States.

NEW JERSEY.

LEWIS MORRIS.

LIPPINCOTT'S

CABINET HISTORIES.

NEW JERSEY.

PHILADELPHIA.
J. B. LIPPINCOTT & Co
1856

THE

HISTORY OF NEW JERSEY

FROM ITS

Earliest Settlement to the Present Time.

EDITED BY

W. H. CARPENTER,

AND

T. S. ARTHUR.

PHILADELPHIA:
J. B. LIPPINCOTT & CO.
1856.

STEREOTYPED BY L. JOHNSON AND CO.
PHILADELPHIA.

PUBLISHERS' PREFACE.

THERE are but few persons in this country who have not, at some time or other, felt the want of an accurate, well written, concise, yet clear and reliable history of their own or some other state.

The want here indicated is now about being supplied; and, as the task of doing so is no light or superficial one, the publishers have given into the hands of the two gentlemen whose names appear in the title-page, the work of preparing a series of CABINET HISTORIES, embracing a volume for each state in the Union. Of their ability to perform this well, we need not speak. They are no strangers in the literary world. What they undertake the public may rest assured will be performed thoroughly; and that no sectarian, sectional, or party feelings will bias their judgment, or lead them to violate the integrity of history.

The importance of a series of state histories like those now commenced, can scarcely be estimated. Being condensed as carefully as accuracy and interest of narrative will permit, the size and price of the volumes will bring them within the reach of every family in the country, thus making them home-reading books for old and young. Each individual will, in consequence, become familiar, not only with the history of his own state, but with that of other states: —thus mutual interest will be re-awakened, and old bonds cemented in a firmer union.

In this series of CABINET HISTORIES, the authors, while presenting a concise but accurate narrative of the domestic policy of each state, will give greater prominence to the personal history of the people. The dangers which continually hovered around the early colonists; the stirring romance of a life passed fearlessly amid peril; the incidents of border warfare; the adventures of hardy pioneers; the keen watchfulness, the subtle surprise, the ruthless attack, and prompt retaliation—all these having had an important influence upon the formation of the American character, are to be freely recorded. While the progressive development of the citizens of each individual state from the rough forest-life of the earlier day to the polished condition of the present, will exhibit a picture of national expansion as instructing as it is interesting.

The size and style of the series will be uniform with the present volume. The authors, who have been for some time collecting and arranging materials, will furnish the succeeding volumes as rapidly as their careful preparation will warrant.

CONTENTS.

CHAPTER I.

CHAPTER II.

CHAPTER III.

CHAPTER IV.

CHAPTER V.

CHAPTER VI.

CHAPTER VII.

CHAPTER VIII.

CHAPTER IX.

CHAPTER X.

CHAPTER XI.

2

CHAPTER XII.

CHAPTER XIII.

CHAPTER XIV.

CHAPTER XV.

CHAPTER XVI.

CHAPTER XVII.

CHAPTER XVIII.

CHAPTER XIX.

CHAPTER XX.

HISTORY OF NEW JERSEY.

CHAPTER I.

New Netherland—Traffic with the Indians—Settlement on Manhattan Island—Argall's visit to Manhattan—The States General grant commercial privileges to discoverers—Block explores the harbour of New York—Coasts with Christiaanse, Connecticut and Rhode Island—Manhattan Island fortified—May enters the Delaware Bay—Authorities appointed to govern New Netherland—Alliance with the Iroquois—Increase of population at New Amsterdam—The Plymouth settlement—Dutch West India Company organized—A colony planted on the Delaware—Fort Nassau built—Administration of Minuits—Commercial prosperity of New Netherland—New plan for colonization adopted—Manors of Pavonia and Swanandael—De Vries's settlement at Hoarkill—Offence given to the Indians—Massacre of the colonists—Return of De Vries—Abandonment of the Swanandael purchase.

ALTHOUGH discovered by a navigator in the service of a Dutch company, the territory adjacent to the Hudson River was not formally claimed by Holland until after the lapse of several years. In 1610, a few merchants of Amsterdam fitted out a ship with various sorts of merchandise, and despatched it to the newly-found lands, in order to open with its native inhabitants a traffic in furs, which were there both abundant and cheap. Success attending this venture, similar voyages became frequent, and trading-houses began to spring up on Manhattan Island, and at Beaverwyck, where Albany now stands.

Antagonistic as these establishments were to the pretensions of England, they did not long remain unnoticed by that country's agents in America. In November, 1613, Captain Argall, of Virginia, while returning from an unjust and useless expedition against the French in Acadia, visited the feeble trading-post at Manhattan, and compelled the Dutch to stipulate allegiance to Great Britain, tribute to Virginia, and the partial payment of his own expenses. But no sooner had Argall left the bay than the Dutch flag was again hoisted, and every thing went on as before.

In April following this occurrence, the States-General of Holland issued a decree, granting to such persons as should discover new lands, the right of exclusive trade to them for four successive voyages. In order to secure the benefits of this grant, a number of merchants entered into partnership, and fitted out five ships, the chief command of which they gave to Hendrick Christiaanse, with Captains Adrien Block and Cornelius Jacobsen May as his subordinates.

Block was the first to reach the Bay of New York, where, his ship being accidentally destroyed by fire, he built a small yacht, and passed through the East River into Long Island Sound. Near Cape Cod he encountered Christiaanse, returning from Massachusetts Bay, and together they examined the shores of Connecticut and Rhode Island with considerable care and thoroughness.

Immediately on their arrival at Manhattan, a rude fort was erected on the southern extremity of the island; and, in the following year, a small redoubt was thrown up on the opposite bank of the Hudson, probably at the present Jersey City Point.

May extended his researches farther south. Sailing along the eastern coast of New Jersey, he rounded the cape that now bears his name, and entered and explored the lower waters of Delaware Bay.

In the ensuing autumn a special grant was made to the merchants by whom Christiaanse had been employed, dignifying their simple partnership with the title of "The United New Netherland Company," and confirming the privileges promised by the previous decree of the States-General. It was now that the name New Netherland was first applied to that part of the continent lying between Cape Cod and the Delaware Bay. Christiaanse, as Upper Hoofdt, or chief-commander, was placed at the head of affairs, with Jacob Elckens, at one time a merchant's clerk in Amsterdam, as his lieutenant.

These officers appear to have discharged the duties entrusted to them with judgment and tact. In the summer of 1671 they concluded a formal treaty of peace and alliance with the Iroquois, or Five-Nations, at which the Delawares and Mohicans were also present. This alliance was kept up for many years, and proved of the highest advantage. Meanwhile, settlers were gradually coming into the country, and the little station at Manhattan, which presently took the name of New Amsterdam, began to wear the appearance of a town. Attempts were likewise made to extend the colony; and, in the year following the treaty with the Iroquois, a few traders planted the village of Bergen, the first of white settlements in New Jersey.

Although the charter of exclusive privileges, granted to the New Netherland company, had by this time expired, a brisk trade continued to be carried on with the settlement at Manhattan for several years, under special licenses to individual enterprise. The benefits of the lucrative traffic of the new country were thus opened to a larger number, but yet with little advantage to its growth into a permanent colony.

In the mean time, a body of English Puritans, who had fled from persecution at home to the more tolerant institutions of Holland, becoming dissatisfied with their residence in the Low Countries, determined to seek some new land, where they might avoid the less austere manners of the Dutch, and still be free to practise and teach the faith they professed. The glowing description given by Sir Walter Raleigh, of Guiana, first drew them toward that country; but, wishing to retain their national character and language, they finally decided upon procuring a patent for lands from the London or South Virginia Company.

Accordingly, on the 6th of September, 1620, after having completed their arrangements, they made their final embarkation at Plymouth, on board the Mayflower, for the new world. Their voyage was long and perilous. Buffeted about by adverse winds and currents, they were compelled to land a considerable distance north of where they intended, and entirely without the limits of the patent they held. Resolving to remain, however, on the 20th of December they began to erect their dwellings of hewed logs, and the town of New Plymouth quickly sprung up on the shore of Cape Cod Bay. The colonists soon after procured a charter from the Plymouth council, which had superseded the old company of that name, and to which the British crown had granted, in total disregard of the Dutch claim, all that part of the American continent, extending from the middle of New Jersey to the Bay of Chaleurs.

Designing to make the settlement on the Hudson the basis of a more extended American colonization, the States-General of Holland, in the year following the landing of the Pilgrims, authorized the formation of the celebrated West India Company, to the means of which they largely contributed, thus giving it the weight and character of a great national association.

To this company it was determined to commit the care of New Netherland, with an exclusive privilege of trade and settlement therein. That territory was at the same time formally erected into a province, to be known and distinguished by certain armorial insignia.

The new company sent out their first ship in 1623, under the command of May, with a number of colonists, and a large store of provisions, merchandise, and arms. Having landed a portion of his passengers and cargo at New Amsterdam, May sailed to the Delaware River, where it was proposed to plant a colony. He chose a spot on the eastern shore, near the mouth of Timber Creek, a few miles below the present city of Camden, and there built Fort Nassau. Leaving a small body of men as a guard for the infant settlement, May returned to the Hudson, high up which Fort Orange was soon afterward built, on the present site of Albany.

In the following year, Peter Minuits, a native of Wesel, in Westphalia, arrived at New Amsterdam, to act as governor, or commercial director of the colony. Under his administration, which lasted till 1631, affairs glided on smoothly, and, in a commercial point of view, prosperously. Lands were now purchased from the Indians; among others, the whole of Manhattan Island, for sixty guilders, or about twenty-four dollars. 'The fort at New Amsterdam was enlarged, and that place made the capital of the colony. The trade of the province was extended, even to the Indians upon the St. Lawrence; and in the first four years it increased one-half, while the income derived from it was full a third more than the outlay of the company.

In 1627, Minuits, for the first time, held communication with the Puritans, now firmly established at Plymouth, after six years of wearisome effort. Letters were sent to the governor of New Plymouth, congratulating him and his people upon the success of their adventure, and proposing a friendly intercourse and trade. Governor Bradford and his council answered in courteous language, expressing their lasting remembrance of the kindness they had received while in the native country of the Dutch. With regard to the proposal for commercial intercourse, they said that "it was very acceptable to them, and they did not doubt but that in a short time they might have profitable trade together." In concluding, however, they plainly intimated their doubt as to the validity of the title of their neighbours to the lands they were then occupying; and requested them "to forbear to trade with the natives in the bay and river of Narraganset," as, "otherwise, they were resolved to solicit his majesty for redress, if by any means they could not help themselves."

To this the Dutch replied firmly, yet with unruffled calmness, insisting upon the justness of their claim, and declaring their determination to uphold it.

The good feeling between the two colonies does not appear to have been interrupted by this difference; for but a short time elapsed when De Razier, second in command at New Amsterdam, was sent, with much pomp and ceremony, as special envoy to the English. The Pilgrims were greatly pleased with the appearance and demeanour of the Dutch envoy, who, on his part, was equally gratified at the manner of his reception and entertainment. Yet he was unable to procure any definite treaty with the English, they urging that, in the then doubtful condition of the title to New Netherland, a matter so important should be arranged by the ministers of their respective nations.

As yet the colonization of New Netherland

had increased but slowly. In 1629, a scheme to promote the peopling of the country was adopted by the directors of the West India Company, and sanctioned by the States-General. A charter of privileges and exemptions was drawn up, under which any person, who within four years planted in New Netherland a colony of fifty souls, above the age of fifteen, might acquire, by purchase from the Indians, as an "eternal heritage," and with the title of patroon, or lord of the manor, a tract of land extending sixteen miles along one side of a navigable stream, or half that distance on each bank, and reaching as far inland as he deemed necessary. With the approbation of the director and council of the province, all other persons, emigrating on their own account, were free to take up as much land as they could properly cultivate. The company was pledged to protect the colonists of every degree and condition, from "outlandish and inlandish wars and powers," and to furnish the manors with negro slaves, if the traffic were found profitable. At the same time it reserved to itself the trade in furs, and monopolized the sale of woollen, linen, and cotton fabrics, by prohibiting their manufacture in the colony.

Even before this charter was ratified by the States-General, two of the directors of the company, Godyn and Bloemart, prepared to secure a portion of the advantages it offered, by commissioning their American agents to purchase from the resident chiefs, a slip of land two miles wide, and extending from Cape Henlopen to the mouth of the Delaware River. On the 5th of May, 1630, a second tract, sixteen miles square, and comprising Cape May with the adjacent country, was purchased on behalf of the same individuals. Staten Island, and the country around Hoboken, under the name of Pavonia, were soon after taken up for the Director Pauw, while Kilian Van Rensselaer became the proprietor of a considerable territory along the Hudson, from Albany to the mouth of the Mohawk.

Naming their purchase Swanandael, or the Valley of Swans, Godyn and his associates at once prepared to colonize it. An expedition was fitted out, under the direction of David Peterson De Vries, an experienced navigator, who had been admitted into the company. Sailing from the Texel, in December, 1630, De Vries, after a quick passage, landed at Hoarkill, now Lewistown, on the western shore of the Delaware Bay, where he built a trading-house and fort, and planted a colony of thirty-four persons. Having remained in the country more than a year, he returned to Holland for supplies, leaving the infant settlement under the care of one Giles Osset. Meantime, Pauw and Van Rensselaer had secured their claims to patroonships, by sending out a number of colonists to settle on their respective tracts.

De Vries had left the Delaware but a little while, when Osset began a quarrel with the Indians, on account of one of their chiefs having taken a plate of tin, stamped with the arms of Holland, from a post in Swanandael, to which it had been fastened, as a token of the claim and possession of the Dutch. Foolishly construing this light trespass into a national insult, Osset so harassed the Indians for redress, that, to get rid of his importunities, they brought him the offender's head. The Dutch commandant was shocked at this unexpected and sanguinary result, and told the Indians that he had wished for no such severity, intending to punish the delinquent with nothing but a simple reprimand. Though they had themselves condemned and executed the offending chief, his friends now plotted a terrible retribution upon the strangers, to whose exactions they attributed his death. Taking advantage of a time when all the colonists but Osset and a single sentinel were labouring in the fields, at a distance from the fort, the savages entered it, bearing packs of furs, and offered to trade. Unsuspicious of evil, Osset ascended to the upper store-room of the fort, in order to get some articles of merchandise, to exchange for the peltries of the Indians. As he came down stairs again, a warrior cleft his skull with a tomahawk, and he fell dead without a groan. The sentinel was next despatched. From this scene of blood the Indians now sauntered out to the fields, greeting the labourers in a friendly way. Mixing freely with their intended victims, they suddenly fell upon them, and in a few moments not one was left alive.

When, in December, 1632, De Vries returned from Holland, he found no white man to welcome him to the shores of the Delaware. The bones of his friends were bleaching in the fields, and the dwellings they had erected were reduced to ashes. His proffered friendship at length induced a few doubting and trembling savages to come on board his ship, and from them he heard the details of the sad fate that had befallen the little colony. Policy, as well as the natural kindness of his heart, led De Vries to overlook the offence of the Indians; and, having distributed presents among them, he formed a treaty of peace and reconciliation. Landing a number of emigrants, he soon afterward sailed in search of provisions, as high up the river as Cooper's Creek, where he narrowly escaped destruction from the treachery of the savages. Deeming the creek a convenient place to attack him, they directed De Vries to bring his vessel into it, pretending, at the same time, they had there the articles he needed. But, as he had been forewarned by an Indian woman of the snare that was laid for him, he avoided it, and returned down the river to Fort Nassau, which now swarmed with savages, the garrison having deserted it nearly two years previous. Many of the Indians came on board the ship, offering beaver-skins for sale. Telling them that the Great Spirit had acquainted him with their evil designs, De Vries compelled the whole party to go on shore. Several of the principal chiefs now collected on the bank of the river, and signified their wish to form a treaty of friendship, to which the mild and peaceful leader of the Dutch readily acceded. To confirm the new treaty, the Indians, according to their custom, made him many presents, but would accept none in return, saying that they did not give presents with the view of receiving others.

Finding it impossible to obtain sufficient provisions on the Delaware, De Vries soon afterward set sail for Virginia, where he met a kindly reception, and was supplied with all he wanted. Returning to the scene of his unsuccessful attempt at colonization, he took on board the few settlers he had left, and made his way to New Amsterdam.

CHAPTER II.

Dispute between the patroons and the West India Company —Manors of Pavonia and Swanandael abolished—Wouter Van Twiller governor—Difficulties with the Plymouth colony—Rival trading-houses on the Connecticut—Governor Kieft—Minuits founds a Swedish colony on the Delaware—Its prosperous condition—English settlers at Salem Creek—Dispossessed by the Swedes and Dutch—Printz succeeds Minuits as governor of New Sweden—Encroachment of the Puritans upon territory claimed by the Dutch—War with the Indian tribes on the Raritan—Unsuccessful negotiations for peace—Massacre of the Indians—Their terrible retaliation—Overtures for peace—Council at Rockaway—War renewed—Settlements on the Passaic destroyed—Captain John Underhill—His successful descents upon Long Island —Arrival of reinforcements—Vigorous prosecution of the war—Interposition of the Mohawks—Peace declared—Unpopularity of Kieft—His recall—Lost at sea.

In the mean time, a sharp quarrel had sprung up between the patroons and the West India Company; the former claiming an exclusive right to trade within the limits of their respective territories, while the latter contended for a monopoly in the fur traffic, and charged the patroons with having grasped at undue advantages, by purchasing such extensive and favourably located tracts. A long and serious dispute resulted, and it was finally settled only by abolishing the manors of Pavonia and Swanandael.

During the progress of this quarrel, Governor Minuits "fell into disputes with the company," the consequences of which were his displacement and recall to Holland. His successor, Wouter Van Twiller, formerly a clerk in the employ of the West India Company, arrived at New Amsterdam in the spring of 1633.

During the five years that Van Twiller was governor of New Netherland, but little worthy of historical notice occurred. Several new trading-posts were established, and the fur traffic extended, while many improvements were made and farms opened on the island of Manhattan. It was during this period, however, that the good feeling hitherto existing between the Manhattanese and their Plymouth neighbours gave way to the jealousies created by commercial rivalry; and, at the close of Van Twiller's administration, both the Dutch and the English, in defiance of each other's remonstrances, had built trading-houses and begun settlements on the Connecticut River. About the same time a few English, under the leadership of one Captain Holmes, attempted to plant a colony in the neighbourhood of Fort Nassau, but being discovered by the Dutch, the whole party were made prisoners, and carried to New Amsterdam.

Van Twiller having fallen under the suspicion of being more faithful to his own interests than to those of the province, the West India Company, in March, 1638, notified him of his dismissal from office, and appointed William Kieft to be his successor.

The new governor was a man of great energy, but passionate and overbearing, and with little of the cool decision necessary to carry him well through the difficulties that soon on all sides beset his administration.

One of his first acts was to issue a sharp protest against the English plantations on the Connecticut. Treating this remonstrance with silent contempt, the English went steadily on with their settlements. Kieft was illy prepared to resist with any thing more forcible than words, and so endured, as best he could, the aggressions he was not able to prevent.

Scarcely a month afterward, a new competitor for the territories claimed by the Dutch as a portion of New Netherland, appeared on the waters of Delaware Bay.

As early as 1626, Gustavus the Great, of Sweden, had cherished the design of planting a colony in America; but the subsequent war with Germany, and the death of the Swedish monarch, delayed its execution for many years. In 1633, however, the project was revived by Oxenstiern, the enlightened chancellor of Christina, the daughter and successor of Gustavus.

Indignant at having been removed from his office, Minuits, the former governor of New Netherland, now offered his services to conduct the Swedish enterprise. Oxenstiern did not long hesitate to accept his offer, and two ships, the Key of Calmar and the Griffin, were presently made ready and placed under his orders. Sailing in these two vessels, well provided with a a store of provisions and merchandise, the little colony of Swedes and Fins arrived off Cape Henlopen, or, as they called it, Paradise Point, early in the spring of 1638. Having purchased the lands from this point to the falls at Trenton, they formed a nucleus for their contemplated settlement, by building a fort near the mouth of Christiana Creek, on the western shore of the Delaware. Kieft immediately issued a sharp remonstrance against the new colony, declaring that it occupied lands which the Dutch had already studded with their forts, and sealed with their blood. Determined to remain, the Swedes made every preparation to defend themselves; but Kieft, with unaccountable forbearance, went no further than to authorize the erection of a fort at Lewistown.

As time glided by, the Swedish colony on the Delaware increased and prospered. Vessels were continually arriving, crowded with emigrants from the bleak plains and rugged hills of Scandinavia. Though the Dutch regarded the settlement with a jealous eye, they made no attempt to disturb it for many years; and, on one occasion, at least, they and the Swedes leagued together against the encroachments of the English.

In 1641, while Sir Edmund Ployden was vainly endeavouring to settle his Palatinate of New Albion, comprising the country from Maryland to Connecticut, a company of nearly fifty families sailed from New Haven, to plant a colony upon the Delaware. They finally disembarked upon the banks of what is now Salem Creek, a few miles above its mouth, and began to clear fields and erect houses. Van Gessendam, the Dutch commandant at Fort Nassau, sent notice of these intruders to Kieft, who immediately despatched two vessels with orders to reduce or disperse the colony.

Equally watchful, the Swedish commandant had marked the English when they entered the bay; and, with a view to dispossess them of the territory they had occupied, he sent an agent to purchase the whole tract from its Indian owners. When the expedition fitted out by Kieft made its appearance, the Swedes joined with the Dutch, and they presently proceeded together to the English settlement, took the colonists prisoners, burned their houses, and confiscated their goods.

Minuits having died about this time, Colonel John Printz succeeded him as governor of New Sweden, arriving in the Delaware on the 16th of February, 1643. Landing upon the island of Tennekong, or Tinicum, a few miles below Philadelphia, he built, with huge hemlock logs, the Fort of New Gottenburg, around which the houses of the emigrants who had accompanied him soon began to cluster.

While the Swedes were setting up their authority over the Dutch possessions on the Delaware, the English continued to narrow the limits of New Netherland upon the north. At any other time, it is probable that Kieft would have disputed every inch of the ground with the intruders; but Indian disturbances had broken out, and he was now fully occupied in contending with an enemy that seemed bent upon his destruction.

This desperate and sanguinary contest began in the summer of 1640. Having been charged with the commission of a few petty thefts, the Indian tribes upon the Raritan were visited by a party of Dutch soldiers, and several of their leading chiefs subjected to insult and gross maltreatment. The maddened savages, in the following year, retaliated by murdering the settlers and laying waste the plantations on Staten Island. Not long afterward a Dutchman was slain by an Indian of the Raritan tribe, who, when a boy, had witnessed the murder of a kinsman by the whites, and had sworn to avenge it. The offender's nation having refused to deliver him up, they were outlawed, and a price set upon their heads. During the following year they evinced a disposition to yield, and steps were taken toward a treaty of reconciliation. But, while these negotiations were pending, an Indian, the son of a chief, was made drunk and then robbed by some Dutch traders. Furious from a sense of the wrong he had suffered, and blinded by intoxication, the savage took revenge by shooting down the first white man that fell in his way. Expressing their grief for this unfortunate occurrence, a deputation of chiefs waited upon Kieft, and offered to compound the murder by paying a fine of two hundred fathoms of wampum. The governor was inexorable, and demanded the fugitive; but the Indians were unable or unwilling to surrender him.

Contrary to the advice of the pacific De Vries, Kieft now determined upon an exterminating war against the savages. Imitating the cunning of those he plotted to destroy, the governor kept from them every intimation of the evil that was impending, and directed a continuance of kind intercourse with them, "until God's will and proper opportunity should be offered." That opportunity came in February, 1643.

Descending from their strongholds in the north, a war-party of the Mohawks made an onslaught upon the tribes around Manhattan, and compelled them to seek the vicinity of the Dutch for protection. Many of the colonists were disposed to pity them, and gave them food; but Kieft, seizing the chance, joined with their foes, and determined upon their destruction. Accordingly, on the night of the 25th of Februaro, a party of soldiers was sent across the Hudson to Pavonia, where a large number of the trembling fugitives had collected. The Indians were sleeping without guards, and in no expectation of evil. Their surprise was complete, and scarcely a hatchet was raised in defence. Eighty of their number, men, women, and children, were cruelly massacred. "This was a feat," wrote De Vries, "worthy the heroes of old Rome—to massacre a parcel of Indians in their sleep, to take the children from the breasts of their mothers, and to butcher them in the presence of their parents, and throw their mangled limbs into the fire or water! Other sucklings had been fastened to little boards, and in this position they were cut in pieces! Some were thrown into the river, and when the parents rushed in to save them, the soldiers prevented their landing, and let parents and children drown." During the same night a second party of soldiers fell upon the Indians at Corlear's Hook. No mercy was shown. Forty miserable savages were butchered in cold blood; some while sleeping, others while flying without a show of resistance; and many, having crawled away in the darkness, were found at day-break, stiffened with wounds, and put to death.

Kieft gave the returning troops an exulting welcome, and liberally rewarded them for their services. But his triumph was brief. The exasperated savages inflicted a terrible retaliation. Discovering that the massacres they had at first attributed to their enemies, the Mohawks, were in reality committed by the whites, they sallied out in every direction, and, in a few days, almost depopulated the country around Manhattan. Villages were burned, farms desolated, men and women murdered, and children carried into captivity. The Dutch colony was brought to the brink of ruin; and, in their terror, all the inhabitants that could, sought safety by a return to Holland.

Kieft was now compelled to sue for peace. Satisfied with the vengeance they had inflicted, sixteen sachems of the Long Island tribes consented to meet a deputation of the colonists, at Rockaway, on the 5th of March, 1643. Having assembled around the council-fire, one of the chieftains presently arose, holding in his hand a bundle of little sticks, and thus addressed the Dutch envoys:

"When you first arrived on our shores, you were destitute of food; we gave you our beans and our corn; we fed you with oysters and fish;

and now, for our recompense, you murder our people."

With these words the orator laid down one stick, thus indicating that this was his first charge. Continuing, he said:

"The traders whom your first ships left on our shore to traffic till their return, were cherished by us as the apple of our eye: We gave them our daughters for their wives: among those whom you have murdered, were children of your own blood." Having concluded his second complaint, the chief put down another stick, while many remained in his hand, to show the number of accusations that were still to come.

Through the influence of Roger Williams, the Long Island sachems finally agreed upon a truce, and a month later, the Raritan and other river Indians likewise came to terms. Peace, however, lasted but a little while. It was hard for the savages to forget the injuries they had sustained—one had lost a father; a second, a mother; many, their children, kinsmen and friends; they still nursed the hope of revenge. "The presents we have received," said an old chief, mournfully, "bear no proportion to our loss—the price of blood has not been paid.'

At length the discontent of the tribes broke out in a fresh war. In September a detachment of soldiers were taken prisoners, and in the following month the settlements near the mouth of the Passaic were laid waste. Affairs now became even more serious than they were in the previous disturbances. Driven from their plantations, the terrified colonists collected in the immediate neighbourhood of Fort Amsterdam, where for nearly two years they lingered, sometimes on the brink of starvation, and momentarily fearing an attack that would end in their extermination.

But whatever may have been the faults of Kieft, he did not lack spirit. Soon as the war was renewed, he bestirred himself to save the colony. Having vainly applied to the authorities of Connecticut for assistance, he hired Captain John Underhill, an English soldier, already famed as an Indian fighter, to take command of the Dutch troops. With a little army of one hundred and twenty men, Underhill entered upon a series of fierce and energetic measures. Partially beaten at times, and on other occasions seriously harassed, the courage of the Indians began to give way. Closely following up his lesser triumphs, Underhill, in 1644, made two sanguinary descents upon Long Island—in the first, killing near a hundred savages, and taking many prisoners; while, in the second, he attacked an Indian town, set fire to it, and put to death five hundred of the inhabitants, who had assembled to celebrate one of their yearly festivals.

With these victories the hopes of the colonists began to return. The Indians were weary of being hunted like wild beasts, and several of the tribes sued for peace. At length the West India Company were enabled to send a reinforcement of troops to Manhattan, and Kieft determined upon a vigorous prosecution of hostilities. At this moment the Mohawks interposed, and sent an envoy to their friends, the Dutch, to exert his influence in favour of peace. His mission succeeded. Delegates from the tribes of New Jersey, and other hostile nations, met in council with the authorities of New Netherland, in front of Fort Amsterdam, and on the 30th of August, 1645, a solemn treaty put an end to the war.

The rejoicings of the colonists on this occasion were great, and they set apart a day for public praise and thanksgiving. Yet the memory of the troubles they had endured, and the losses they had suffered, pressed heavily on their minds, and fostered a desire for the removal of Kieft, whose rash and barbarous policy had involved them in so much difficulty. Complaints of his mismanagement at length reached the West India Company. Finding that their own interests would be advanced by a change of governors, they finally sent out a recall to Kieft, and in the fall of 1647 he embarked for Holland. Encountering a furious storm, the ships in which he sailed was dashed ashore on the coast of Wales, and the merciless governor, together with some eighty companions, was swallowed up in the waves.

CHAPTER III.

Governor Stuyvesant—His character—His wise and cautious policy—Quarrel with New England—Belligerent desires of Stuyvesant—The West India Company counsel peace—Negotiations opened—Provisional treaty concluded—Second English attempt to found a colony on the Delaware frustrated—Swedish colony threatened by Stuyvesant—Fort Cassimir constructed—Printz builds Fort Elsingburg—Rising governor of New Sweden—Takes Fort Cassimir by stratagem—The Swedes conquered by Stuyvesant—Indian hostilities—Activity of Stuyvesant—Prosperous condition of New Netherland—Lord Baltimore claims the territory on the west bank of the Delaware—Its cession to the city of Amsterdam—Perilous position of Stuyvesant—Stringent regulations of the West India Company—Concessions demanded by the people—Haughty reply of Stuyvesant—A popular assembly established—New Netherland granted to the Duke of York—Arrival of the English fleet—Stuyvesant summoned to surrender—Capitulation.

In May, 1647, the governor appointed to succeed Kieft arrived at New Amsterdam. His name was Stuyvesant, a brave and experienced soldier, honest, frank, and tolerably learned, but somewhat haughty in his bearing toward the poorer classes, of whom he did not profess to hold a very high opinion. Before receiving his present commission he had held the office of vice-director at Caraccas, where his services had been such as to gain him the good regards of the West Indian Directory.

The new governor promptly applied himself to averting the dangers which on all sides threatened his province. Taught by the calamities of his predecessors, he wisely adopted a gentle and forbearing policy in his dealings with the natives, thus keeping the period of his administration almost undisturbed by Indian wars. His chief concern, however, was centered in the doubtful attitude assumed by the English and by the Swedes.

Immediately after Stuyvesant's arrival, the commissioners of New England addressed him a letter of congratulation, concluding with an earnest appeal for reparation of the injuries they had received from Kieft. Without justifying all the acts of Kieft, Stuyvesant made a counter-claim for redress, and demanded a restoration of the Dutch territories on the Connecticut. The old territorial quarrel was thus renewed in all its bitterness. Already involved, the question now became more and more knotty, with little or no prospect of its happy solution. Never having admitted the title of the Dutch to any territory in America, the New England men extended their settlements, even threatening to occupy the banks of the Hudson. Protests and counter protests drew hard words from both parties; and the fiery Stuyvesant would probably have resorted to arms, but the West India Company, to whom he applied for authority and assistance, earnestly counselled peace. "War," said they, "cannot in any event be to our advantage; the New England people are too powerful for us."

Negotiation being the only course left him, Stuyvesant repaired to Hartford, where a convention of delegates, representing the interests of both nations, was presently held. After a series of lengthy discussions, on the 19th of September, 1650, a provisional treaty was concluded, making the boundary between the two colonies, to begin at Greenwich on the main, and at Oyster Bay, on Long Island. This intercolonial treaty received the sanction of the States-General, and of the West India Company, but was never ratified by the British crown.

The claim of the New Haven people to lands on Salem Creek was still undecided, and they now attempted for the second time to plant a colony in that region. Commissioned by Governor Eaton, who gave them a friendly letter of explanation to Stuyvesant, a little company of emigrants sailed from Connecticut River for the Delaware, early in the spring of 1651; but stopping at Manhattan to deliver their message to Stuyvesant, they were arrested, and obliged to return to New Haven, whence they immediately addressed a petition to the New England commissioners, begging them to protect their persons and property, and to maintain "the honour of the English nation." Choosing rather "to suffer affronts for a while, than to seem to be too quick," the commissioners would not commit themselves at that time, inasmuch as the governor of New Netherland had signified his determination to resist, at all hazards, every attempt to plant colonies upon the land in dispute.

Uneasy at the progress of the Swedish settlements upon the Delaware, Stuyvesant now bent his efforts in that direction. For the protection of the Dutch commerce, already suffering from the restrictions imposed upon it by the Swedes, he built Fort Cassimir, near the mouth of Brandywine Creek, and not more than five miles from Christiana. Having issued an unheeded protest against this movement, Printz, who was still governor of New Sweden, built Fort Elsingburg, a little distance below, on the eastern bank of the Delaware; but a great swarm of musquitoes presently falling upon the garrison, they were compelled to evacuate the newly-erected works.

The proximity of Fort Cassimir to the Swedish garrison at Christiana, led to a series of petty quarrels, which were kept up until 1654, when John Rising, now governor of New Sweden, combining stratagem with a superiority in force, mastered the Dutch troops, and took possession of their fort. This grievous insult awoke the ire of the West India Company, who directed Stuyvesant to "revenge their wrong, to drive the Swedes from the river, or compel their submission." Collecting a force of six hundred men, Stuyvesant appeared in the Delaware, in September, 1655. He first assailed and took Fort Elsingburg, which the Swedes had again occupied. Forts Cassimir and Holy Trinity were next reduced, and finally the victorious Dutch compelled the submission of Gottenburg, the capital of New Sweden, where Rising himself commanded. Honourable terms were granted to the vanquished Swedes, the peaceable possession of their estates being assured to them, upon condition that they would acknowledge the authority of the States-General. Thus fell, never to rise again, the only colonial establishment of Sweden in the New World.

Upon his return from the Delaware, Stuyvesant found the colonists in a wretched state of terror and despondency. Taking advantage of the absence of so large a number of the warlike inhabitants, the river tribes in the vicinity of Manhattan had collected a fleet of over sixty canoes, laid waste the neighbouring farms, and even appeared in hostile array before New Amsterdam. But the presence of Stuyvesant infused fresh courage into the breasts of the Manhattanese, and prompt and active measures were taken, which soon restored the colony to hope and confidence.

It was now that for a time the Dutch were permitted to rejoice in the possession of New Netherland. Quiet and prosperity seemed at last to have crowned their efforts. Their power in America was apparently fixed upon a permanent foundation. But scarcely had this hope been entertained, when new dangers began to threaten their existence. The partially settled dispute with the New England colonies broke out with additional asperity; and, while Stuyvesant was engaged in that direction, a fresh quarrel sprung up with the English in the south, who were preparing to wrest from his authority the lately-acquired territory of New Sweden.

On the restoration of Charles II. to the throne of Great Britain, in 1660, Lord Baltimore, the proprietary of Maryland, insisted upon a right he had previously urged, to the whole territory claimed by the Dutch, westward of the Delaware River. Declaring that they had bought and colonized the lands in dispute long before Lord Baltimore's patent was in existence, the West India Company refused to yield up their possessions, and avowed their firm resolve "to defend them, even to the spilling of blood." At length, fearful of encroachments from the south, they transferred the whole colony, extending from the falls at Trenton to Cape Henlopen, to the city of Amsterdam.

At the same time, Massachusetts was claiming the Pacific for her western boundary, while Connecticut advanced step by step toward the Hudson. Stuyvesant saw the peril of his position. "Alas!" he wrote to the West India Company, "the English are as ten to one in number to us, and are able to deprive us of the country when they please." Resorting again to negotiation, he repaired in person to Boston, but effected nothing. A similar diplomatic mission to Hartford was equally barren of good. The English would not acknowledge the right of New Netherland to any American territory at all.

While thus New Netherland was threatened with dangers from without, the internal condition of things was illy calculated to foster a genuine public spirit. Unwise in their conceptions of government, the West India directors would allow no security for popular rights and privileges, such as were enjoyed by the people of New England. Clinging to arbitrary power, they insisted on making the laws of the colony, appointing its officers, and deciding all its controversies. Little alteration had been made in the original plan of government, and such changes as were wrought by the growth and widening interests of the province, related wholly to commercial privileges, and not to political enfranchisement. Transplanted to New Netherland by emigrants from the English colonies, the notion of popular freedom took deep root in the minds of the people of the province, and they entered into an earnest struggle to ameliorate their political condition. A convention met at New Amsterdam, in 1663, and, among other things, demanded that the people should share in the enactment of those laws by which they were governed. Having exhausted his arguments against this demand, Stuyvesant, who had but little faith in "the wavering multitude," commanded the convention to separate, under a threat of severe punishment. "We," said the proud governor to the retiring members, "We derive our authority from God and the West India Company, and not from the pleasure of a few ignorant subjects." And in this haughty and overbearing assumption he was fully sustained by the company. "Have no regard to the will of the people," said they, in their instructions; "let them no longer indulge the visionary dream that taxes can be imposed only with their consent." But the desire of the people for political freedom was not to be easily rooted out; and many were found willing to yield quietly to English rule, if they could but obtain a share in the rights and privileges of their Puritan neighbours.

It was when the colonists were in this state of indifference, that dangers began to thicken around New Netherland. Conscious that it was now necessary to create a spirit of patriotism, Stuyvesant became more and more willing to enlarge the privileges of the masses, and in 1663 he conceded a poplar assembly. But the concession came too late to effect its object. Rumours of a threatened invasion from England found the people still indifferent, and disposed to shift upon the West India Company all care for the integrity of the province.

At length rumour became certainty. Disregarding the claims of Holland, Charles II. of England, in the year 1664, granted to his brother James, Duke of York and Albany, a patent for territories in which was comprised the province of New Netherland. An armament, consisting of three ships, with one hundred and thirty guns, and six hundred men, was immediately made ready, and sent to take possession of the countries named in the patent to the Duke of York. Colonel Nicholls, who had served under the celebrated Turenne, was placed in command of the invading force, with authority to act as governor of the province when it should be subjugated. Having touched at Boston, where instructions were left to raise a body of troops to join the expedition, the fleet sailed for the Hudson River, and arrived in front of New Amsterdam on the 27th of August, 1664.

Soon as the English armament appeared, a deputation from Stuyvesant and the city bore a letter to Nicholls, desiring, "with all respect and civility," to know the motive of his presence. The British commander replied by demanding of Stuyvesant the immediate recognition of English sovereignty, at the same time offering security to the lives, liberties, and estates, of all who would quietly submit.

Though greatly outnumbered by the English, Stuyvesant was yet loth to surrender without a struggle. At the first rumour of the designs of Britain, he had spiritedly proposed that every third man should be called into service, "as had more than once been done in fatherland." And now, when summoned to surrender, he invited the burgomasters and council of the city to meet him, and vainly endeavoured to infuse into them some portion of his own martial spirit. But, believing that they would in the end be conquered, the peaceful burghers could see no use in prolonging a contest, which might cost them much blood and treasure, with no corresponding return. They asked to see the summons of the English commander. Knowing that they would eagerly accept the terms it offered, Stuyvesant hesitated and then refused. Again and again they urged their request, when, enraged at their importunity, the passionate governor tore the letter in fragments, and dashed it at the feet of the startled burghers.

For several days longer, Stuyvesant sturdily held out—now negotiating, and again assuming an attitude of defiance. Nicholls had threatened to inflict the horrors of war, in case of a refusal to surrender. "Touching your threat," was Stuyvesant's undaunted reply, "we have nothing to answer, only that we fear nothing, but what God, who is just and merciful, shall lay upon us, all things being in his gracious disposal; and we may as well be preserved by him with small forces as by a great army—which makes us to wish you all happiness and prosperity, and to recommend you to his protection." But this show of confidence was of little avail; and, at length, beset by dissensions within, and a numerous enemy without, the old governor reluctantly consented to terms of honourable capitulation. The remaining forts on the Delaware and Hudson soon after surrendered, and the whole of New Netherland fell quietly into the possession of England.

CHAPTER IV.

The Duke of York's patent to Berkeley and Carteret—The province of New Jersey—Liberal policy of the proprietaries—Their concessions to popular freedom—Nicholls governor of New York—His activity in colonizing New Albania—Carteret appointed governor of New Jersey—Establishes his capital at Elizabethtown—Inducements held out to settlers—Rapid increase in population—Puritan settlement on the Passaic—Threatened by the Hackensack Indians—Peace restored—Newark founded—Narrow policy of the colonists from Connecticut—First legislative session of New Jersey—Partial adoption of the harsh New England code—Local rights of self-government claimed—Opposition to quit rents—Great disaffection throughout the province—A new assembly constituted—Deposition of the governor—Carteret sails for England—Carteret's authority confirmed—Power of the assembly curtailed—War between England and Holland—Capture of New York by the Dutch—Its restoration to the English.

NEARLY two months previous to the conquest of New Netherland, the Duke of York, in consideration "of a competent sum of money," had assigned to Lork Berkeley and Sir George Carteret, favourite courtiers of the king, all that portion of the province lying westward of Long Island, and bounded on the west by the Delaware, on the east by the Hudson and the main ocean, and on the north by the forty-first degree and fortieth minute of latitude. To this region was given the name of Nova Cæsaria, or New Jersey, out of compliment to Carteret, who, in 1649, had gallantly defended the little Isle of Jersey, of which he was then governor, against the forces of the Long Parliament.

The first care of the proprietaries was to people their province. Wisely foreseeing that a policy favourable to popular freedom would best promote that end, they drew up and published, as the fundamental law of the colony, a paper of "Concessions and Agreement," the general tone of which was highly liberal. To all actual settlers they offered tracts of land, varying in extent from sixty to one hundred and fifty acres, according to the time of their arrival in the province, and to the number of their bound servants and slaves. An annual quit-rent of a half-penny the acre was to be required for their allotments after the year 1670. A governor and council of twelve, nominated by the proprietaries, and an equal number, at least, of representatives chosen by the people, were to constitute the legislative assembly. The enactments of this body were to be subject to the approval of the proprietaries, who also reserved to themselves the appointment of judicial officers. No taxes were to be levied, except with the authority and consent of the colonial assembly. Freedom of conscience and worship was guarantied to all citizens, provided that freedom was not used "to licentiousness, and to the civil injury or outward discomfort of others." Ample provision was made for the support of clergymen, to be appointed by the colonial assembly; but permission was at the same time allowed the colonists to associate for the maintenance of such ministers as they might prefer.

The territory thus erected into a province, with such security for the liberties of its settlers, was then scarcely more than an uninhabited wilderness. Its native population was by no means large, and consisted of a few scattered clans of the inoffensive Delawares. With the exception of the little hamlet of Bergen, nothing that could be called a town had resulted from the various attempts to establish European settlements. In the neighbourhood of Bergen, and along the western shore of Newark Bay, the plantations of the Dutch were numerous, while here and there, through the present counties of Gloucester and Burlington, a few Swedish farmers had built their cabins, and cleared lands for cultivation. At Long Point, opposite Mattinicunk Island, where Burlington now stands, three Dutch families had established themselves, forming the largest collection of civilized habitations in all West Jersey.

Immediately after the surrender of New Netherland, Nicholls assumed the government of the province, as lieutenant of the Duke of York.

Ignorant of the transfer of New Jersey, he prepared to colonize the eastern portion of it, to which he gave the name of Albania. With his sanction, an extensive territory, bordering upon Newark Bay, was purchased from the Indians by a few New England Puritans, who settled on it during the year 1664. In the spring of 1665 a similar patent was issued, under the same sanction, for the country from the mouth of the Raritan to Sandy Hook; and, before Nicholls could be informed of the change of ownership, he was able to congratulate himself, that, "on the new purchases from the Indians, three towns were already beginning."

The hasty zeal of Nicholls to colonize his cherished Albania, "preferable to all the remaining tracts," led to long and tedious litigation, which seriously disturbed the tranquillity of the province for more than half a century.

Meanwhile, Philip Carteret, a brother to one of the proprietaries, having been commissioned as governor of New Jersey, was making preparations to depart for the western world. Sailing from England in the ship Philip, and accompanied by about thirty emigrants, he arrived in the province some time during the month of August, 1665. Carrying in his hand a hoe, to remind his little company of the design that had brought them across the ocean, he landed at a place to which the name of Elizabethtown was presently given, in honour of the kind-hearted Lady Carteret. Four families from New England had already made here one of the "beginnings" spoken of by Nicholls, who now warmly urged the Duke of York to revoke the grant, by which, without knowing it, he had given away the fairest portion of his province. But it was too late. Satisfied with the freedom they enjoyed, the colonists did not second his appeals. The independent existence of New Jersey was secured.

Having elevated his little village of log huts to the dignity of a provincial capital, Carteret actively bestirred himself to augment the population and prosperity of the colony under his charge. Messengers were sent abroad to set forth the happy situation of the province, the liberality of its institutions, the cheapness of its lands, the richness and fertility of the soil along its rivers, its mild and healthy climate, the peaceful character of its few aboriginal inhabitants, and its nearness to long-established colonies, by which the distresses of an adventurer into a new country would be done away with. Seconded by all these recommendations, the efforts of Carteret were followed by surprising success. From New England, Long Island, and from Great Britain, the province soon received large additions to its population. Elizabethtown, and then Middletown and Shrewsbury, all founded before the coming of Carteret, grew up into thriving villages, the two latter still retaining certain local powers of self-government which had been granted to them by Nicholls. No less thriving were the settlements of Piscataway and Woodbridge, established during the year 1666, by emigrants from New England.

Early in the same year, an association of church members, from three several towns in Connecticut, sailed into the Passaic, and landed at a point previously selected, "beyond the marshes lying to the north of Elizabethtown." Scarcely had the emigrants brought their goods from shipboard, when a party of Hackensac Indians appeared on the ground, claiming the soil as their own, and insisting that it should be paid for before the settlement could go on. Having selected the tract in expectation that Carteret was authorized to extinguish the Indian title, the disheartened colonists prepared to abandon their enterprise; but, at the earnest request of the governor, they agreed to hold a council with the natives, from whom they purchased the territory comprising more than one-half the present county of Essex, paying for it in goods and wampum, valued at about one hundred and forty pounds, New England currency. Having thus settled their difficulty with the Indians, the emigrants immediately began to erect a town, to which they presently gave the name of Newark. Constituting themselves on the narrow and intolerant principle of withholding certain political rights from all persons not subscribing to the doctrines "of some one of the Congregational churches," they resolved, "with one heart and consent," "to carry on their spiritual concernments, as well as their civil and town affairs, according to God and a godly government;" and to be ruled "by such officers as the town should annually choose from among themselves," under "the same laws as they had in the place from whence they came."

The influence of the Puritan emigrants was felt in the first assembly of New Jersey, which commenced its session at Elizabethtown, on the 26th, and closed on the 30th of May, 1668. Transferring the main points of the New England codes to the statute-book of the province, a bill of pains and penalties was passed, closely copying the heretical law, and making twelve crimes, under certain circumstances, punishable with death. But little additional business was completed, several bills being left over to the ensuing session, which opened on the 3d of November in the same year. During this session no acts of importance were carried through, from a want of harmony between the two branches of the assembly. There were besides other signs of approaching trouble. Resting on the ground of their local rights of self-government, the towns of Shrewsbury and Middletown now denied the authority of the assembly, by refusing to allow the collection of certain taxes which had been levied in accordance with an enactment of the previous session. As they had been represented in the popular branch, this proceeding was a singular one, and showed far more independence than consistency. Having refused to take the usual oaths of allegiance to the province, their deputies to the second meeting of the assembly were refused admittance. Here the matter appears to have rested for a time; but other and greater troubles were soon to follow.

For nearly eighteen months afterward, however, affairs went on with tolerable smoothness, and the province continued to increase in population and importance. But when the first payment of the quit-rents was called for, on the 25th of March, 1670, the smothered discontent of the colonists broke out in violent opposition to the demand. Foremost to treat the claim of the proprietaries with contempt, were the early settlers of Elizabethtown. They had come into the country, with the sanction of Nicholls, before the transfer of New Jersey to its present proprietors. They had purchased their lands from the Indian and rightful owners of the soil, and the title they had thus acquired was, according to their notions, far superior to any right the proprietaries could have. Consequently, they would pay no quit-rents. Other settlers, who had arrived in the province at a later period, pretended to class themselves with these; and in a short time the whole colony was in a tumult of litigation. For two years matters continued to grow more and more confused, until the political condition of the province was almost one of complete anarchy.

In May, 1672, the disaffected colonists even went so far as to constitute a new assembly, by which body the proprietary governor was displaced, and a successor appointed in the person of James Carteret, a worthless natural son of Sir George. Proclamations were immediately issued against this proceeding, but they availed nothing. All power had gone over to the usurper. At length, finding his authority disregarded, his officers imprisoned and their estates confiscated, the governor followed the advice of his council, and proceeded to England, leaving John Berry to act as deputy in his absence.

At the request of the proprietaries, the Duke of York soon after sent out a letter unfavourable to the claims of the colonists. This was followed by one from the king, confirming the authority of Carteret, and requiring obedience to the officers appointed by the lords' proprietors. New "concessions" were also drawn up, somewhat curtailing the original powers of the assembly, by transferring to the governor and council the sole right of approving such ministers as might be nominated by the several towns, and of regulating the meetings and adjournments of the legislature.

At the same time a period was fixed of three years from 1673, at the expiration of which all quit-rents were to be paid up, and the malecontents to submit to the terms of the proprietaries. But, before the appointed time came round, war broke out between England and Holland. The States-General immediately despatched a small squadron to harass the commerce of the British colonies. Having captured many English traders homeward-bound from Virginia, they determined to attempt the re-capture of New York. Governor Lovelace was absent, and Captain Manning, with a company of regulars, in command of the fort. At the first summons of the Dutch, who appeared before New York late in July, 1673, Manning surrendered. Exercising moderation in the hour of their triumph, the forces of the States-General easily gained the submission of the remaining parts of the province. New Jersey, and the settlements on the Delaware, quietly followed their example, and New Netherland again enjoyed a momentary existence.

Having thus reconquered their American colony, the Dutch immediately prepared a code of mild and liberal laws for its regulation. But scarcely had the new code gone into general operation, when peace was concluded between Holland and Great Britain, on the 9th of February, 1674. By the sixth article of this treaty, a mutual restoration of conquests was agreed upon; and, on the 31st of the following October, New Netherland was finally transferred to England.

CHAPTER V.

The Duke of York confirmed in his title to New York—Andros appointed governor—Petition of New Jersey—The Quakers punished as recusants—Unjust charges against them—Their principles proscribed—Their persecution in England—Advised to settle in America—Salem settled—Governments of Fenwicke and Carteret—The boundaries of East and West New Jersey established—Constitution promulgated—Its liberal concessions—Emigration of wealthy Quakers—Anecdote of Charles II.—Difficulty with Andros, governor of New York—Burlington settled—Fear of Indian hostilities—A special treaty entered into—Speech of an Indian sachem—Progress of the colony—Increase of population.

UPON the final relinquishment of New Netherland by the United Provinces, the Duke of York procured a new patent from the king, in order to quiet certain doubts that had arisen with regard to the validity of his title, which the previous surrender to the Dutch was thought to

6*

have impaired. Two days after this patent was executed, on the 1st of July, 1674, the duke commissioned Edmund Andros as governor of New York and "its dependencies." These included "all the lands from the west bank of Connecticut River to the eastern shore of Delaware Bay."

Much trouble subsequently resulted from this commission, and it has been thought that the duke, while conferring it, designed to revoke his grants to the New Jersey proprietaries. But, if such was his dishonourable intention, he lacked resolution to fulfil it; for toward the end of the same month he renewed the title of Sir George Carteret to a moiety of the province, of which an informal partition was at this time made. Previously, on the 18th of March, 1673, Berkeley, now an old man, disappointed in his hopes of colonial aggrandizement, had sold out his share to John Fenwicke and Edward Byllinge, for the sum of one thousand pounds.

Both these purchasers were members of the Society of Friends, or Quakers, a religious body destined to exercise an important influence over the settlement and future character of the province.

Arising in England in 1644, at a time when men's minds were more than usually disposed to active inquiry into the deeper questions of religion as well as of civil government, the sect of people called Quakers soon became distinguished for the spirit and boldness with which they conducted their investigations. Nor was the pure and genuine piety of much the greater part of the new community considered less remarkable. There were many others, however, who, mistaking their own wild impulses for the direct promptings of the Holy Spirit, frequently committed acts justly to be called extravagant, offensive to the proprieties of life, and not wholly without injury to the public peace.

The mad zeal of these enthusiastic visionaries finally brought them in collision with the state authorities, and during the last years of Cromwell's protectorate, severe measures were taken against them. Punished rather as religious "recusants," than as offenders against the public peace, it was not long before they could claim the merit of suffering for conscience' sake. But persecution only increased their numbers and inflamed their zeal.

Soon after the restoration of Charles II., this persecution was renewed, though the members of the society were now inclined to disavow their connections with these fanatics, to whom they presently gave the name of "Ranters." Notwithstanding the plain and unequivocal teaching of their founder, that it was unlawful to use carnal weapons in advancing spiritual objects, they were unjustly charged with holding to the doctrine of the Millennarians, or Fifth Monarchy Men, that even force might be employed in overturning those temporal powers, supposed to be in the way of the coming spiritual and divine dominion.

Under this impression Charles proscribed their principles as being "inconsistent with any kind of government," and a sharp law was enacted against them as "an abominable sect."

The king himself early changed the hasty and mistaken opinion he had formed of the Quakers, for a truer and more liberal view of their doctrines. He even entered into a familiar and intimate acquaintance with some of their prominent leaders. But this did not soften the rigour of the penal enactments against them. Harassed on all sides by special statute, by the general laws against dissenters, and by the statute against Roman Catholics, they were thrown into the foulest dungeons, scourged, exiled, sold into colonial bondage, stripped of their estates, and even deprived of life itself by the carelessness or inhumanity of their jailers.

It was when this persecution was at its height that George Fox, the founder of the Society of Friends, returned to England from a missionary tour through the American colonies.

To testify to their faith, the Quakers shrank from no suffering, however great. Some, in the exuberance of their zeal, were willing to court it.

But the more quiet members of the society were of the opinion that to avoid persecution without abandoning the tenets of their religion, was not to be judged as wrongful. It is probable that on his return to England, Fox represented to them the advantages to be enjoyed under the tolerant constitution of New Jersey, where they might hope for peace and security in the practice of their faith. Preferring voluntarily expatriation to a forced exile, numbers immediately prepared to escape to the land thrown open to them by the sale already noticed.

Understanding that Carteret was to retain the northern part of the province, Fenwicke and Byllinge determined upon colonizing the southwestern portion along the Delaware. Two years passed away, however, before any settlement was made. Meantime, a sharp quarrel sprung up between the new purchasers with regard to their respective interests in the territory. Shunning the scandal of a law-suit, they left the decision of the question to William Penn. Penn's award was finally acceded to, after some hesitation on the part of Fenwicke, who received one-tenth of the purchase as his share.

Byllinge, failing in business soon after, was obliged to transfer his interest for the benefit of his creditors, to Penn, Gawen Laurie, and Nicholas Lucas. With the concurrence of Fenwicke, these trustees presently divided the whole proprietorship into one hundred shares, of which the ninety belonging to Byllinge were offered for sale.

Matters having been thus arranged, in 1675, Fenwicke, with a large company and several families, set sail from London, in the ship Griffin. A short and pleasant passage brought the adventurers into Delaware Bay, on the eastern shore of which, at its head, they landed near the site of one of the old Swedish forts. From the fair and peaceful aspect of the place, they gave the name of Salem to their new settlement. Having purchased lands from the natives, Fenwicke proceeded to portion them out among the several emigrants, and took upon himself the authority of the province.

Early in the same year, Philip Carteret quietly resumed the government of his kinsman's share of the province. By postponing the payment of the quit-rents, he induced the colonists to accept without murmuring, and even with an appearance of satisfaction, the new and less popular concessions sent out by the proprietary.

In November, the second regular assembly met. Having adopted several measures for the well-being and orderly management of the colony, they concluded their session with an act of amnesty and free pardon to all persons concerned in the late disturbances.

Early in 1676, the assembly again convened,

but nothing of historical importance was passed. With the exception of some slight symptoms of dissatisfaction with regard to the quit-rents, affairs went on smootmy, and there was a prospect of long-continued quiet.

At length, on the first of July, a formal division of New Jersey was agreed to by Carteret. From the ocean, at Little Egg Harbour, a line was drawn to a point on the Delaware River, in the neighbourhood of forty-one degrees north latitude; the country north and east of which remained in the possession of Carteret, with the title of East New Jersey, while the other section was assigned in severalty to the Quaker proprietaries, under the title of West New Jersey.

Meanwhile, these proprietaries had prepared in England, a code of fundamental laws for the province. "We lay," wrote Penn and his colleagues to the colonists, "we lay a foundation for after ages to understand their liberty as Christians and as men, that they may not be brought into bondage but by their own consent; for we put the power in the people."

The Quaker "concessions and agreements" were first made public on the 3d of March, 1676. Entire freedom of conscience, universal suffrage, and voting by ballot were fully established. None could be imprisoned for debt. Orphans were to be educated at the public expense. "All and every person in the province" was, "by the help of the Lord and these fundamentals, to be free from oppression and slavery." Humane and just regulations were framed to protect the native inhabitants against encroachments. No attorney or counsellor was required in the management of courts. For the government of the province, the people were to elect an assembly, each member of which was to be paid one shilling a day, "that he might be known as a servant of the people." The chief executive power was confided to ten commissioners, to be chosen by the assembly. That body was also to appoint the judges, who retained their offices but two years, sitting in court only as assistants to the jury, in which, alone, resided the authority to make decisions, whether as to the law or the fact.

Such are the main features of the first political constitution drawn up by members of the Society of Friends. While many may point out defects, the instrument, viewed as a whole, is yet worthy of hearty approval and commendation. Far in advance of any system of government then in existence, it contrasted favourably with that even of the eastern province, which was avowedly popular and concessive. To its framers may justly be awarded no slight participation in the honour of having laid the foundation of civil and religious freedom in the new world.

Pursuant to the plan of the concessions, Thomas Olive and others were presently appointed as commissioners, to superintend the colony, to which two companies of emigrants, principally wealthy Friends from Yorkshire and London, were already prepared to remove.

During the summer of 1677, these commissioners, accompanied by a large body of settlers, embarked on board the ship Kent, at London. While the vessel was anchored in the Thames, preparatory to sailing, the king chanced to come by in his pleasure-barge. Remarking the plain garb of the men of peace, Charles came alongside, and, having learned that they were all Quakers, destined for the colony of New Jersey, he blessed them, and gave them his good wishes.

After a long and tiresome passage, the Kent was brought to anchor within Sandy Hook, from which place the commissioners proceeded on a visit to the governor of New York. Received with all courtesy by Andros, they informed him of their design. Claiming jurisdiction over New Jersey, Andros demanded whether they had a warrant from the Duke of York. On their answering in the negative, he refused to recognise their authority. They offered to remonstrate. Pointing significantly to his sword, the arbitrary governor intimated the extent to which he would oppose them. The peace-loving commissioners were silenced. Finally, however,

Andros gave them a warrant from himself, until the matter could be referred for decision to England.

Meanwhile, the main body of the colonists had entered the Delaware. Procuring interpreters from among the Swedish settlers planted near the present site of Swedesborough, they purchased from the Indians three large and contiguous tracts of land, extending from Old Man's Creek to the falls at Trenton.

Two distinct settlements were at first proposed, but it was finally determined to join together and form one town. Accordingly, on the tract between Rancocas Creek and the falls, a town was presently laid out, to which the name of New Beverly was first applied, then Bridlington, and afterward Burlington, which it still retains. A main street having been cleared, along this the settlers began to erect their dwellings, the Yorkshire proprietors on the eastern side, and those from London on the west.

Winter was wellnigh over before these houses could be made habitable. In the mean time the settlers sheltered themselves in rude huts, built in imitation of the wigwams of the natives. For a meeting-house, a tent of sail-cloth was early set up. Under this the Quakers began to hold religious union.

The simple-hearted savages in the neighbourhood were unusually kind to the new comers, supplying them plentifully with corn and venison. Hostilities were subsequently threatened by the Indians, on the ground that the strangers had sold them the small-pox along with certain match-coats. Apprehending trouble, the colonists sought the assurance of a special treaty, and a peace-council was shortly held with the Indian kings, under the shades of the Burlington forests. The English having made known their fears, an old sachem rose, and, speaking for his brethren, said :—

"Some of our young men may utter such words as neither you nor we approve. We cannot help that. You cannot help it. We are your brothers. We have no mind to make war. When we have war we are but skin and bone. The meat that we eat doth do us no good. The kind sun cannot shine upon us, for we then hide us in holes and corners.

"When we intend to make war upon you, we will let you know of it, and the reason; that whatever wrong you have done us may be repaired. If you give us no satisfaction, then we will make war. You, likewise, will act in this way with us. Otherwise, there should be no war.

"You are our brothers, and we wish to live like brothers with you. We will leave a broad path for you and us to walk in. If an Indian is asleep in this path, the Englishman shall pass by and do him no harm. If an Englishman falls asleep in this path, the Indian shall pass him by, and say, 'He is an Englishman; he is asleep; let him alone; he loves sleep.' The path shall be plain; there shall not be in this path a stump to hurt the feet.

"As to the small-pox, it came in the time of my grandfather; it came in the time of my father; and now in my time it is come." Then stretching his hands toward heaven, he continued, "I do believe that it is the Man above that hath sent it to us."

A good understanding having been established with the Indians, by this and subsequent councils, the colony soon assumed a thriving appearance. Constant accessions were made to the number of its inhabitants. In November, 1677, the ship Willing Mind, from London, landed about seventy emigrants, some of whom settled at Salem, others at Burlington. She was soon after followed by the fly-boat Martha, with one hundred and fourteen passengers from Yorkshire. On the 10th of December, of the succeeding year, came the Shields, from Hull. Gliding up the Delaware, with a fair and fresh breeze, her passengers admired the surrounding country, and especially pointed out, as a "fine spot for a town," the lands upon which Philadelphia has since arisen. Passing by this, the gale swept them on to Burlington, so far as which no vessel had hitherto sailed. Mooring that night to a tree in front of the town, her astonished passengers, on the following morning, walked ashore, with the hard frozen river beneath their feet.

CHAPTER VI.

Dispute between New York and East New Jersey—Arbitrary conduct of Andros—Claims jurisdiction over New Jersey—Carteret refuses to resign his government—His arrest—Tried at New York and acquitted—Andros attempts to control the assembly of East New Jersey—Their spirited response—Heavy tax on imports—Remonstrance of the New Jersey proprietaries—Their complaints referred to commissioners—The tax pronounced illegal—The Duke of York relinquishes his claim to govern New Jersey—Byllinge governor of West New Jersey—Appoints Jennings deputy-governor—First legislative assembly convenes—Adoption of a constitution—Burlington erected the capital of the province—The assembly maintains its prerogative—Amendment of the constitution—Jennings elected governor—Is sent to England—Olive governor—Byllinge appoints John Skene deputy-governor—Death of Byllinge—Sale of his interest in New Jersey—Dr. Coxe claims entire executive control—A change foreshadowed.

While the Quaker colony was settled under auspices which promised a fair prospect of rapid and substantial growth, difficulties were springing up in East New Jersey, that in the end, for a while, disturbed the tranquillity of the whole province.

To foster a spirit of commercial enterprise among his people, Governor Carteret prepared to open a direct trade with England, unencumbered by custom. Opposing what he styled an infringement of his master's rights, Andros, then governor of New York, ordered that no ship should land on the Jersey shore, until it had first paid an impost duty at Manhattan. On the death of Sir George Carteret, in 1679, he took a bolder step, and claimed jurisdiction over the province. Recurring to the terms of his original commission, he called upon Carteret to lay down his authority. Unexpected as this demand was, the governor maintained a fearless and unshaken front. "It was by his majesty's command," he replied, "that this government was established. Without that command, it shall never be resigned but with our lives and fortunes."

On the 7th of April, 1680, Andros, attended by his councillors, and a few leading merchants of New York, presented himself at Elizabethtown. Courteously received by Carteret, he at once unfolded to him the object of his visit, and endeavoured to induce him to resign his government. Finding all his arguments vain, he somewhat abruptly withdrew, warning the inhabitants that if they did not comply with his demand, the peril would rest upon them alone.

Regardless of the hospitable welcome he had

received, Andros, on the 30th of April, despatched a file of soldiers to Elizabethtown, to capture Carteret. Entering the governor's mansion at a late hour of the night, they dragged him rudely from his bed, and carried him, bruised and maltreated, to New York, where he was kept in close confinement until the 27th of the following month.

On that day Andros summoned a special court, himself being chief justice. When placed on trial, Carteret fearlessly avowed that he had refused to surrender his authority. He then demanded his release on parole, and protested bitterly against being tried by a court, of which his accuser was also judge. When the jury returned with a verdict of "Not guilty," Andros, with violence of language, charged them anew, and ordered them to reconsider their verdict. Twice was this scene renewed; but the jury, faithful to their duty and their honour, persisted in finding an acquittal. Carteret, however, was detained in custody until the controversy could be decided in England.

At once taking advantage of this virtual deposition, Andros again entered East New Jersey and appeared before its assembly. His power was such as to awe its members; but they evinced no disposition to yield to his arbitrary will. He endeavoured to intimidate them by exhibiting the king's patent to the Duke of

York. "We are the representatives of the freeholders of this province," was their reply. "His majesty's patent, though under the great seal of England, we dare not grant to be our rule or joint safety; for the great charter of England is the only rule, privilege, and joint safety of every free-born Englishman." Their answer breathed the firmness of freemen, and the independence of New Jersey remained intact.

Andros did not confine his usurpations to the eastern province. Denying the West Jersey proprietors any right of jurisdiction, as early as 1676, he had imprisoned Fenwicke, the founder of Salem, for claiming the government of his share of the province; and had liberated him only upon his promise not to assume any authority on the eastern shore of the Delaware. This outrage was repeated in 1678, it being alleged that Fenwicke had violated his word.

Other difficulties soon sprung from the same source. Pretending that the duke's authority extended over the whole of Delaware Bay, Andros levied a tax of five per cent. on all English goods imported into the colony. The payment of these customs was rigidly enforced. No exemption was permitted "to the smallest vessel, boat, or person."

Provoked beyond endurance, the proprietors earnestly and often importuned the Duke of York for redress. At length, rather wearied by the reiteration of these complaints than moved by their justice, he consented to refer the question to disinterested commissioners, who finally submitted it to the decision of Sir William Jones, a leading lawyer of that day.

On behalf of the colonists, the Quaker proprietaries prepared an elaborate argument. It was worthy the founders of a free state. After deducing their title, they say:—

"An express grant of the powers of government, and that only, induced us to buy the moiety of New Jersey; for the government of any place is more inviting than the soil; and what is good land without good laws? If we could not assure people of an easy, free, and safe government, liberty of conscience, and an inviolable possession of their civil rights and freedoms, a mere wilderness would be no encouragement; for it were madness to leave a free and improved country to plant in a wilderness, and give another person an absolute title to tax us all." Stating the tax imposed by Andros, they continue:—

"For this we make our application to have speedy redress, not as a burden only, but as a wrong. Tell us by what right are we thus used? The King of England cannot justly take his subjects' goods without their consent. This needs no more to be proved than a principle; it is a home-born right, declared to be law by divers statutes.

"To give up the right of making laws, is to change the government, and resign ourselves to the will of another. The land belongs to the natives; of the duke we buy nothing but the right of an undisturbed colonizing, with an expectation of some increase of the freedoms enjoyed in our own country. But what gain has it been to us, that now pay an arbitrary custom, neither known to England nor to New York, and those other plantations? We have not lost any part of our liberty by leaving our country.

"The tax is a very surprise to the planters. It is paying for the same thing twice over. Custom laid upon planting is unprecedented. Besides, there is no end of this power; for, since by this precedent we are assessed without law, and excluded from our English rights of common assent to taxes, what security have we for any thing we possess? We can call nothing our own, but are tenants-at-will, not for the soil only, but for our personal estates. This sort of conduct has destroyed governments, but never raised one to true greatness.

"Lastly, to exact such an unterminated tax from English planters, and to continue it after so many repeated complaints, will be the greatest evidence of a design to introduce, if the crown should ever devolve upon the duke, an unlimited government in Old England."

Such, briefly, but in their own language, was the argument of the proprietors. It was successful. Sir William Jones decided that the tax was illegal. His decision was sustained. The Duke of York acquiesced in it, and, in 1681, made a new and separate grant of West New Jersey to the trustees, relinquishing all claim to the territory and the government.

With this success the peace of West New Jersey seemed to be confirmed. Numerous settlers, mostly Quakers, continued to flock into the province. All went on smoothly.

Finding it inconvenient to leave England, Byllinge, who had been elected governor by the proprietaries, appointed Samuel Jennings, a man of some distinction already in the province, to be his deputy. On the 21st of November, 1681, Jennings convened the first legislative assembly. Having adopted a code of "Fundamental Constitutions," strictly in accordance with the liberal spirit of "the concessions," the assembly proceeded to enact six and thirty laws for the well-ordering of the province. For defraying the expenses of government, they ordered a levy of two hundred pounds, to be paid in corn, or skins, or money. A heavy penalty was imposed upon the sale of ardent spirits to the Indians. In all criminal cases—murder, treason, and theft excepted—it was provided that the person aggrieved might pardon the offender either before or after condemnation.

During the following session, held in May, 1682, Burlington was erected into the capital of the province. That town and Salem were established as ports. To provide for that class of bound-servants who, to procure the means of coming to the country, had indentured themselves to the more opulent colonists, it was enacted that every such person might claim from his master, at the expiration of his indenture, a set of agricultural implements, necessary articles of apparel, and ten bushels of corn.

When the assembly again met, in 1683, a question of considerable importance was brought under deliberation. Byllinge, as proprietary, claimed, and had already exercised, the power of nominating the deputy-governor. From the first, his right to do so had been questioned, and the subject had excited no little discussion. As an intimation of his design to maintain this right, Byllinge appears to have resolved upon the removal of Jennings. The dissatisfaction of the colonists with a claim to any authority not springing from themselves, now came rapidly to a crisis. Besides, they were pleased with Jennings, and wished to retain him. Following the advice of Penn, the assembly amended the constitution according to the prescribed method, and then elected Jennings as governor.

At a subsequent session, Jennings was deputed to proceed, with a coadjutor, to England, to negotiate upon this subject with Byllinge. Before departing he nominated Thomas Olive as his deputy. Presently elected governor, Olive remained in that office until September, 1685. The mission of Jennings was only in part successful. A new and liberal charter was indeed obtained, but Byllinge would not renounce his claim. He soon afterward commissioned John Skene as his deputy. Though the assembly agreed to recognise this commission, it was with the plain reservation that they thereby lost none of "their just rights and privileges."

Byllinge dying in 1687, Dr. Daniel Coxe, of London, already largely concerned in West Jersey, purchased the interest of his heirs in the soil and government. Informing the provincial council of proprietors of what he had done, Coxe presently laid claim to the entire executive control of the colony. Liberally confirming the "concessions" as a favour, he yet left nothing to the people as rights. Probably his energetic revival of the claim of Byllinge would have created more excitement than it did, had not a new and unexpected interference from another quarter suspended, for a time, the exercise of the powers of government, either by Coxe or by the people.

CHAPTER VII.

Quit-rent disputes—East New Jersey purchased by Penn and others—Extension of the partnership—Robert Barclay made governor—Appoints Thomas Rudyard his deputy—Session of the assembly—The province divided into counties—Administration of Rudyard—Gawen Laurie governor—Mixed character of population in New Jersey—Scottish emigrants—Scot of Pitlochie's book—Lord Campbell appointed deputy governor of East New Jersey—James II. violates his obligations—Difficulties with New York—New Jersey threatened—Remonstrance of the proprietaries—Surrender of East and West New Jersey to the jurisdiction of the crown—Andros commissioned governor—Flight of James II.—Resumption of the proprietary governments—Hamilton governor—Land titles—Hamilton superseded by Basse—Interprovincial disputes—Hamilton re-appointed governor—New Jersey becomes a royal province.

In consequence of the decision of Sir William Jones, East New Jersey again reverted to the authority of Governor Carteret. But the quit-rent disputes being revived, the possession of the province seemed likely to prove more troublesome than lucrative. Tired of their responsibility, the trustees of Sir George presently offered his interest in the province for sale.

Encouraged by the success of their plantations on the Delaware, the Quakers of England resolved to secure the opportunity thus offered of widening the field of their enterprise. Accordingly, in the month of February, 1682, William Penn, and eleven associates of the Quaker persuasion, became the purchasers of East New Jersey, for the sum of three thousand four hundred pounds.

Having prepared, for the encouragement of settlers, a brief eulogistic account of the political and natural advantages of the province, each of the twelve new proprietors chose a partner. These were principally Scotchmen, and many were not Quakers. Among them were the Earl of Perth and Lord Drummond, members of the Scottish privy council. As a majority of the five thousand inhabitants already in the colony belonged to other religious sects, this choice of partners was probably made to allay the jealousy with which it was reasonably to be expected that a government composed entirely of Quakers would be regarded. On the 13th of March, 1683, the twenty-four obtained from the Duke of York a new, special, and final patent.

Previously, the amiable and ingenious Robert Barclay, celebrated by his appellation of "the Apologist," himself one of the proprietors, had been appointed governor for life. Permitted to exercise his authority by deputy, he never visited the province. The gentleman he chose as his temporary representative, was Thomas Rudyard, an attorney of some distinction in London. In November 1682, Rudyard arrived in the province, which he found tenanted by "a sober, professing people, wise in their generation, and courteous in their behaviour."

By the assemby, which soon after met, a number of laws were enacted, slightly modifying the character, jurisdiction, and proceedings of the courts, and softening, in some degree, the severity of the earlier criminal and penal codes. The concessions of the late proprietaries were renewed, and the province divided into four counties, Bergen, Essex, Middlesex, and Monmouth.

Rudyard's administration seems to have been productive of considerable harmony among the divided and clashing interests that had hitherto distracted the province. But it was of brief duration. Having quarrelled with Groome, the surveyor-general, Rudyard suspended him from office. The English proprietors, however, sided with Groome; and, though fully aware of the good Rudyard had already effected, they determined upon his removal.

His successor was Gawen Laurie, a Scotchman by birth, a member of the Society of Friends, and a merchant of London. Arriving in the province early in 1684, Laurie immediately bestirred himself to build up the new town of Perth Amboy, so named in honour of the Earl of Perth. A favourite project of the proprietaries, this town had been laid out the previous year, and already contained a few houses. Here it was expected to raise up a great commercial emporium, to rival New York; but the destiny prefigured for the young city has never been realized.

New Jersey still bears evidence to the mixed character of her early population. To the Dutch colonists, New England Puritans, and English Quakers already in the province, a large accession of Scottish Presbyterians was now to be made.

The efforts of Charles II. to bring back Scotland to Episcopacy, had met with no general opposition from the Presbyterians. Under the name of Cameronians and Covenanters, however, a few of their number still persisted in the determination to practise their faith. Rigorously persecuted, in consequence, and hunted like wild beasts, the despairing Covenanters occasionally rose against their oppressors. But every attempt to shake off the yoke of intolerance only recoiled upon themselves with redoubled violence.

In 1683, shortly after the final grant of East New Jersey to the twenty-four proprietaries, a fresh proclamation from the English government proscribed all who had ever communed with the rebellious covenanters. The lives of twenty thousand persons were thus put at the mercy of informers. The insurrection of Monmouth followed. A fearful and bloody revenge was inflicted upon the maddened insurgents. The whole Calvinistic population of Scotland was beset by proscriptions or penalties.

Writing at this time to the East Jersey proprietaries in England, Laurie urged them to hasten emigration. "Here wants nothing but people," he said. "Every proprietor's sending over ten people will bring all the division that hath been here to an end." Governor Barclay and others among the proprietaries were natives of Scotland. From that country efforts were immediately made to draw emigrants to the province. The persecution the people was there suffering, it was thought would induce them to accept readily an asylum beyond the Atlantic. Partial success only followed these efforts. With all they were forced to undergo, the Scots were not easily persuaded to exile themselves from their native land.

The accession of the Duke of York, as James II., to the English throne, in 1685, instead of bringing relief to the persecuted Covenanters, did but aggravate their sufferings. Crowded into prisons, numbers of them perished from thirst and suffocation. Hundreds of unfortunate fugitives, after being tried by a jury of soldiers, were put to death in a body on the public ways. Women were bound to stakes set up in the sea at low water-mark, and there left to be drowned by the swelling waters.

Wearied with persecution, the miserable Covenanters were ready to seek peace by expatriation. It was at this moment that George Scot, of Pitlochie, at the instance of the proprietaries, addressed to his countrymen a book entitled "The Model of the Government of the Province of East New Jersey in America," in which certain objections to emigration were refuted, and the advantages offered by the province set forth in full. "It is judged the interest of the English government," he wrote, "altogether to suppress the Presbyterian principles; the whole force of the law of this kingdom is levelled at the effectual bearing them down. The rigorous putting these laws in execution hath, in a great part, ruined many of those who, notwithstanding thereof, find themselves in conscience obliged to retain these principles. A retreat where, by law, a toleration is allowed, doth at present offer itself in America, and is nowhere else to be found in his majesty's dominions." Doing what he had so well advised others, the author himself, in August, 1685, embarked with his family and two hundred Scottish emigrants, for the shores of East New Jersey.

The result of his little publication was most important and highly beneficial to the colony. Companies of Scotch Presbyterians speedily flocked into the province, in such numbers that, even at the present day, the character they then gave it is not entirely destroyed.

Still further to influence the tide of Scottish emigration, the twenty-four proprietors presently displaced Laurie, and conferred the office of deputy-governor on Lord Neill Campbell. Compromised by some insurrectionary movements in Scotland, Campbell willingly accepted, and, in 1686, came out to the province. His stay, however, was brief. In March of the following year, he sailed again for England, leaving Andrew Hamilton as his substitute.

Every thing promised well for the future of the province. But James, the king of Great Britain, was little disposed to fulfil the engagements he had entered into while Duke of York. Influenced by Dongan, the successor of Andros, he was preparing to wrest from the Jersey proprietaries the rights, powers, and privileges he had but lately, for the third time, confirmed to them. By extending his royal authority over New Jersey, his revenues would be largely augmented, and his cupidity speedily devised a scheme for effecting that object.

To prevent violations of the navigation laws, William Dyer had been appointed by Laurie collector of the customs in New Jersey. His appointment resulted in evil. Scarcely was his authority established, when the inhabitants found themselves obliged to enter their vessels and pay duties at New York. Unjust as it was unpalatable, this regulation was either slighted, or obeyed with hesitation. Dyer immediately complained of the opposition he encountered. With singular promptitude, the English ministry, in April, 1686, answered his complaint by ordering the issue of a writ of *quo warranto* against the proprietaries. New Jersey was threatened with being made "more dependent."

Aroused by this sudden stroke, the proprietaries prepared an earnest remonstrance. But it was vain to appeal to the justice of James. Finding the king immovable, the proprietaries, in 1688, formally surrendered their claim to the jurisdiction of East Jersey, stipulating only for their right of property in the soil. Against West Jersey, where Coxe was still claiming executive authority, a writ of *quo warranto* had likewise been issued. In October of the same year, the province was yielded up, on conditions similar to those stipulated by the eastern proprietaries. Thus all New Jersey, along with New York and New England, was brought under the jurisdiction of Andros, whom James had commissioned as governor.

Noting the quiet compliance with which his arbitrary assumptions had been received, the king was dilatory in making good his acquisition. While the necessary grant of the soil to the proprietaries was yet unexecuted, the Revolution that placed William of Orange on the British throne arrested the completion of the whole design.

On the downfall of the House of Stuart, the proprietary governments of the two Jerseys were quietly resumed. In the eastern province, Hamilton had been confirmed as deputy-governor by Andros. Doubting as to what would be his proper conduct in the changed condition of affairs, in August, 1689, he sailed to England, to consult personally with the proprietaries, leaving the inhabitants to the care of their town and county officers. From this period until 1692, East Jersey had no other government. Quarrelling among themselves, the proprietaries found it hard to exact obedience from their subjects, who rejected two successive governors, appointed after the death of Barclay—one in 1690, the other in the following year.

This difficulty, however, was arranged in 1692, by the selection of Hamilton, the former deputy, who was at the same time commissioned as governor of the western province, where Coxe had finally abandoned all claim to authority.

For the following five years New Jersey enjoyed a period of comparative repose. The old dispute about land-titles, however, was recommenced with considerable bitterness. Carried before the provincial courts, the matter was decided against the claimants under the Indian title. But the subsequent annulment of this decision by a royal council, again laid the subject open to discussion.

Though the administration of Hamilton had proved highly popular, the proprietaries, in 1697, were reluctantly compelled to revoke his commission, in consequence of a late parliamentary enactment, disabling all Scotchmen from offices of public trust and profit.

The successor of Hamilton was Jeremiah Basse. Not having the regular approbation of the king, the advent of Basse into the province was the signal of uproar. A majority of the resident proprietaries would not acknowledge his authority as legal. Thus disowned, Basse sought to strengthen himself by favouring the party hitherto adverse to the proprietary government.

In the midst of the contention that now arose, the illiberality of the neighbouring province of New York created a new cause of trouble. Renewing their claim to supremacy over New Jersey, the assembly of New York attempted to levy a duty on East Jersey exports. Though countenanced by the Board of Trade, the attempt ended in a failure, but not until the dispute had wellnigh ripened into a war between the provinces. It was decided that no customs could be imposed upon the Jerseys unless by their own consent, or by an Act of Parliament.

Meantime, the popular dissatisfaction with Basse continued to grow in strength, until it broke out in complete anarchy. Offenders, who had tumultuously defied his authority, when imprisoned were immediately set at liberty by armed mobs, who forced their way into the jails, assailing and maltreating the officers placed to guard them. At length, finding his situation one of vexation and trouble, Basse returned to England, some time in the summer of 1699.

Hoping to restore tranquillity, the proprietaries re-appointed Hamilton. But it was now too late. Disorderly and seditious meetings assembled, denying the validity of his commission. The judges of his appointing were assaulted in open court by bands of armed men. Sheriffs were attacked and wounded while in the performance of their duties. So great became the confusion, that, in succeeding years, this period was known as that of "the Revolution."

The cause of these disturbances seems to have been the claim of the proprietaries to exclusive possession of the soil, under grants from the Duke of York, and their consequent demand for the payment of quit-rents, and repudiation of such titles as had been derived from the Indians. Apparently viewing the proprietaries as so many extortioners, the disaffected colonists, heedless of what the result might be, earnestly prayed the king to deprive those obnoxious persons of their authority.

At length, embarrassed by their own numbers and conflicting interests, and wearied out with an ineffectual struggle to exercise their seigneurial functions, the proprietaries of both the Jerseys were induced to entertain a proposal from the royal council, to cede their rights of jurisdiction to the crown. Besides, the English Lords of Trade, claiming New Jersey as a royal province, threatened to involve them in an expensive suit with the crown, in order to test the validity of their pretensions.

In such a suit, their chance of success would have been slight. Thus menaced, both from within and from without, they deemed it best to surrender. Accordingly, after a lengthy negotiation, in which they secured to themselves their property in the soil, and their quit-rents, so odious to the colonists, the proprietaries of New Jersey, East and West, formally resigned their "pretended" rights of government, before the English privy council, on the 17th of April, 1702.

Queen Anne, now on the British throne, immediately proceeded to unite the two provinces into one. Their government, along with that of New York, was entrusted to the queen's kinsman, Edward Hyde, Lord Viscount Cornbury, grandson of the Earl of Clarendon.

CHAPTER VIII.

The new constitution for the Jerseys—The legislative power—In whom vested—Slave trade ordered to be encouraged—The judiciary—Arrival of Lord Cornbury—His demand for a permanent salary rejected by the assembly—Cornbury's illegal proceedings—Opposed by Lewis Morris and Samuel Jennings—The assembly wait upon Cornbury with a remonstrance—His response—Retort of the assembly—Conduct of Cornbury censured by the English ministry—His removal—Imprisoned by his creditors—Popular administration of Lovelace—His death—Ingoldsby deputy-governor—War between France and England—Capture of Port Royal.

EMBODIED in the commission and instructions of the crown to Governor Cornbury, the new constitution of the Jerseys was promulgated on the 10th of November, 1702.

Resembling in many respects that of the other royal provinces in America, the system of government thus given to New Jersey was far less favourable to popular freedom than were the proprietary concessions. In the contests between the proprietaries and the people, which had partly led to its adoption, the former had lost nothing but a claim to authority they could never have enforced, while the latter were to lament a serious curtailment of their former civil liberties.

The legislative power of the province was vested in the governor, twelve counsellors, and twenty-four representatives. Appointed by the crown from a list of names supplied by the governor, the counsellors were to be men of "good lives and well affected," "of good estates and ability," and "not necessitous people or much in debt." The representatives, equally divided between East and West Jersey, were each required to possess a freehold of a thousand acres. The laws enacted by the council and assembly were subject to an immediate veto from the governor, and a veto from the crown at any time. The assembly was to meet at the order of the governor, who might adjourn, prorogue, or dissolve it, according to his discretion. No persons were capable of voting for representatives but colonists possessing a hundred acres of land, or personal property to the value of fifty pounds.

Liberty of conscience was granted to all save Roman Catholics. Quakers were allowed to hold office, and their affirmation was to be accepted in lieu of the customary oaths. The especial favour of the governor was invoked for the Episcopacy, and he was "to take care that God Almighty be duly served," and "the blessed sacrament administered according to the rites of the Church of England." Closely following this display of royal interest in the cause of religion, was an injunction to the governor to encourage the traffic in "merchantable negroes," with which the Royal African Company were to supply the province "at moderate rates."

No printing press was allowed, nor the printing of any "book, pamphlet, or other matters whatsoever, without a license." In the formation of the judiciary, the people took no part; the governor, with the consent of his council, instituting courts of law, and appointing their officers. In suits of law, where the value in dispute exceeded a hundred pounds, an appeal was admitted from the provincial courts to the governor and council; and when it exceeded two hundred pounds, ultimate jurisdiction rested in the English privy council.

With the executive, the press, and the judiciary thus at the pleasure of the crown, it was not long before the people of New Jersey became sensible of the abridgment of their liberties. Conscious of being subjected to wrong, they soon began to claim the privileges of their earlier and freer condition.

Lord Cornbury arrived in the province in August, 1703, and personally met the general assembly at Amboy. During the next session, held at Burlington, in September, 1704, the pleasing opinions previously entertained of Cornbury's good qualities, began to be dispelled by the realities of acquaintanceship. Grasping and needy, he demanded an annual salary of two thousand pounds for twenty years. Accustomed to pay but moderate sums for the support of government, the popular branch of the assembly would allow no more than thirteen hundred a year for three years. Cornbury vainly endeavoured to procure an increase. At length, finding the house immovable, he declared it dissolved, and ordered the election of a second, to meet in the following November.

Employing various artifices, Cornbury succeeded in obtaining a large proportion, but not a majority of the assembly. Complete control being thus almost within his grasp, he did not hesitate to adopt the advice of his subservient council, and refused to admit three of the newly-elected members to their seats, on the feigned ground that their estates were not as large as the royal instructions required. By this unjustifiable proceeding he secured a majority of one favourable to his views. Recklessly prodigal in his expenditures, his thirst for money was first to be gratified by raising his salary to two thousand pounds a year. It was to remain at this rate for two years only. A stringent act for the establishment of a general system of militia, which the former assembly had refused to adopt, was now passed, greatly to the discomfort of the Quaker colonists, who were subsequently subjected to harassing and unnecessary prosecutions under its provisions.

During the two following sessions, in 1705 and 1706, no business of importance was transacted. The governor, however, found his supporters dwindling down into an ineffective minority.

It being necessary to call a third assembly, so that his salary might be renewed, Cornbury ordered an election. All his efforts to regain his lost ascendency were of no avail. In the new assembly, which convened in April, 1707, there was an overwhelming opposition, at the head of which were Lewis Morris and Samuel Jennings. The former, from the eastern section of the province, was of an eccentric but liberal mind, and had been twice expelled from the council for his determined opposition to the measures of Cornbury. The latter, coming from West Jersey, was a true-hearted Quaker, the natural quickness and fire of whose temper, prudence restrained and benevolence softened. Both were men of influence, possessing a perfect knowledge of the interests of the province, with the will, ability, and courage to uphold them.

Having met, the house, after a consideration of the public grievances, adopted a petition to the queen, and a remonstrance to the governor.

Following the custom of the day, the assembly waited on Cornbury with their remonstrance, which was probably the production of Morris. Jennings, as speaker, read it audibly, and with deliberation. Briefly, it was as follows:—

"To lay before the governor the unhappy circumstances of this province, is a task we undertake, not of choice, but necessity.

"We think it a great hardship that persons accused of any crime should be obliged to pay court-fees, notwithstanding the jury have found no bill against them. The granting of patents for the exclusive carriage of goods from Burlington to Amboy, we think to be a grievance, contrary to the statute against monopolies. The establishing fees by any other authority than the general assembly, we take to be a great grievance, directly repugnant to *Magna Charta*. The governor's putting the records of the eastern division of this province into the hands of a pretended agent of the proprietors, who has not given security for the faithful keeping of them, is a crying grievance.

"These, governor, are some of the grievances this province complains of; but there are others of a higher nature.

"The governor has prohibited the proprietors' agents from granting warrants for land in the western division of this province. This is a great encroachment on the proprietors' liberties, but we are not surprised at it, for a greater led the way. That was the governor's refusing to swear three members of the last assembly, upon the groundless charges of two of the council. We would not answer the trust reposed in us, were we to decline letting the governor know our extreme dissatisfaction with so notorious a violation of the liberties of the people.

"Considerable sums of money were raised to procure the dissolution of the first assembly, in order to obtain such officers as the contributors might approve. This house has reason to believe that money was given to Lord Cornbury, and did induce him to dissolve the then assembly, and keep three members out of the next. We cannot but be very uneasy when we find by these new methods of government, our liberties and properties so much shaken, that no man can say he is master of either. Liberty is too valuable a thing to be easily parted with. They have neither heads, hearts, nor souls, that are not forward with their utmost power lawfully to redress the miseries of their country.

"We conclude by advising the governor that, to engage the affections of the people, no artifice is needful, but let them be unmolested in the enjoyment of what belongs to them of right."

Sharp and spirited in its tone, this remonstrance lost nothing in its delivery. At the more pointed passages, Cornbury, assuming a stern air of authority, would break in with, "Stop! what's that?" When thus interrupted, the undaunted Jennings, affecting deep humility, would calmly read over again the offensive passages, with greater and more stinging emphasis than before.

The reply of Cornbury was weak and undignified, though no point of the remonstrance was left unnoticed. Denying the truth of some of the charges, he sought to justify others. In an uncalled-for reflection upon the Quakers, he charged them with disloyalty and faction. Singling out Jennings and Morris, he poured upon them the severity of his abuse, declaring them to be "men known to have neither good principles nor good morals."

Cornbury's reply drew a second paper from the house, reiterating and amplifying their former complaints. In regard to his charges against the Quakers, they answered:—"With those persons, considered as Quakers, we have nothing to do. They, perhaps, will think themselves obliged to vindicate their meetings from the aspersions which your excellency bestows upon them, and to show the world how becoming it is for the governor of a province to enter the lists of controversy with people who thought themselves entitled to his protection in the enjoyment of their religious liberties."

Such of them as were members of the house begged leave to answer the governor's charge, in the words of Nehemiah to Sanballat:—"There are no such things done as thou sayest, but thou feignest them out of thine own heart."

Refusing to receive this answer to his reply, Cornbury prorogued the house. Meeting again in May, 1708, they were at length dismissed, and then dissolved, the governor finding that nothing could be obtained from them, without disagreeable concessions upon his part.

This was the last time Cornbury met the assembly of New Jersey. In New York, as in New Jersey, his administration had produced universal dissatisfaction, while the follies and vices he exhibited in private life were such as to create the profoundest disgust. The Lords of Trade, on complaint of the owners of a merchant vessel which he had seized at New York, under some pretence of violations of the Acts of Trade, pronounced his conduct censurable and illegal. Frequent and earnest petitions were poured into the queen for his removal, and, at length, though her cousin, she deprived him of his commission in the year 1709. No sooner was he removed from his office than his creditors cast him into jail, where he remained a prisoner for debt, in the province he had governed, until, succeeding to the earldom of Clarendon, the privilege of peerage set him at liberty. He then returned to Europe, accompanied by the odium which his character deserved, as a mixture of arrogance and meanness, bigotry and intolerance, rapacity and prodigality. But he had accomplished good, though without design. His arbitrary conduct had created and strengthened in both provinces a spirit of freedom, bold and watchful, and already acquainted with the necessity and the methods of resistance.

The liberal and conciliatory conduct of Cornbury's successor, Lord Lovelace, gave hopes of a happy administration. But the pleasant prospect was presently overclouded by the death of the new and popular governor. Ingoldsby, the subservient lieutenant of Cornbury, for a time occupied the station thus left vacant.

For several years war had been waging between France and England. By the incursions of the French and Indians from Canada, the northern provinces had suffered greatly, and, in the year 1709, the immediate neighbourhood of Boston was threatened by a marauding party of the enemy, who attacked and destroyed the town of Haverhill, on the Merrimac, massacreing many of the inhabitants, and dragging others into captivity.

Alarmed at this onslaught, the New England

people begged assistance from the queen. Vetch, a Boston merchant, was sent to England to press the petition. He returned shortly with the promise of a fleet and army, to co-operate with colonial troops in a simultaneous attack on Quebec and Montreal. In pursuance of his instructions, Ingoldsby called upon New Jersey for assistance. With spirited alacrity the assembly voted to raise a certain number of troops. Appropriating three thousand pounds to aid the expedition, they sanctioned the issue of the first paper money in the province.

The expected army from England not arriving, the enterprise was never prosecuted. But Colonel Nicholson, with the provincial levies, planned and executed a successful attack upon Port Royal, by which full possession of Nova Scotia was obtained, on the 5th of October, 1710.

CHAPTER IX.

Arrival of Governor Hunter—His speech to the assembly—His popularity—Invasion of Canada advocated by Nicholson—Organization of the provincial levies—Disastrous failure of the expedition—Treaty of Utrecht—Quaker difficulties in New Jersey—Opposition against Hunter—His success—Provincial demonstrations of regard—Burnet appointed governor—His removal to Massachusetts—Montgomery governor—Petition for a separate government—Administration of Crosby—Of Hamilton—Separation of the Jerseys from the government of New York—Morris commissioned governor—Rapid decline of his popularity—Maintains the royal prerogatives—War declared between England and France—Shirley plans an expedition against Louisburg—Sharp controversy between Morris and the assembly—Death of Morris—Succeeded by Hamilton—Feeble and abortive attempt to invade Canada—Peace of Aix-la-Chapelle.

MEANTIME Ingoldsby had been removed. His successor was Robert Hunter, a Scotchman by birth. Entering life as the runaway apprentice of an apothecary, Hunter had enlisted as a common soldier in the British army, where he gradually rose to military rank. His engaging person and manners had obtained for him the hand of a peeress—his wit and social qualities the friendship of Addison and Swift.

Brief, frank, and soldierly, and concluding with the excellent maxim, that "all power except that of doing good is a burden," his opening speech to the assembly produced an impression eminently favourable. This impression his conciliatory disposition, and open, candid bearing abundantly confirmed, rendering him the object of almost affectionate regard. Supported by the talent and influence of Morris in the council, his administration of ten years glided on with scarcely a noticeable interruption.

Flushed with his success in Nova Scotia, Nicholson repaired to England, to advocate the reduction of Canada. His solicitations obtained from government a fleet of fifty-five sail, and seven veteran regiments from Marlborough's army. This fleet arriving at Boston in June, 1711, Hunter called the New Jersey assembly. Readily answering his requisition, they ordered the levy of a regiment, and appropriated twelve thousand five hundred dollars, in bills of credit, to defraying its expenses.

At the head of about fifteen hundred provincials, from Connecticut, New Jersey, and New York, and six hundred Iroquois, Nicholson prepared, at Albany, to advance upon Montreal. But the combined army and fleet, under General Hill and Admiral Walker, met with a disastrous failure. While entering the St. Lawrence, on their way to Quebec, several vessels were wrecked, and more than eight hundred men drowned. The Quebec expedition being consequently frustrated, Nicholson could not do otherwise than abandon his designs against Montreal.

From this period the operations of both the belligerent nations grew less and less momentous, until hostilities were brought to a close by the Treaty of Utrecht, in 1713.

A new assembly met in April, 1716, in which there was a temporary majority of the old adherents of Cornbury, several of whom had been the most obnoxious members of his council. Daniel Coxe, son of him who has already been noticed as a West Jersey proprietor, was chosen speaker of the house.

By the party now apparently in the ascendant, it was argued that the colonial enactments permitting Quakers to affirm in all cases, had been annulled by a late parliamentary law, by which it was insisted that they should be solemnly sworn before taking public office, sitting on juries, and appearing as witnesses in capital trials. Holding to this construction, the clerk of the supreme court, contrary to a previous ruling of Chief Justice Jameson, refused to administer to grand-jurymen any thing but an oath. Jameson having fined the clerk for contempt, was in turn indicted by the court of quarter sessions. Hunter sided with the judge. The indictment was nullified, and the lawyers who promoted it suspended from practice.

Wearied by a contest with the new house, the

governor prorogued it. About the middle of May, he summoned it to meet him a second time at Amboy. Coxe and his adherents, intending to keep the governor out of his supplies, denounced this call as illegal, and refused to attend, on the ground that every other session was to be held at Burlington. Stating that he but obeyed the orders of his sovereign, Hunter exerted himself to get a house together. He succeeded in obtaining one with a mere majority favourable to his views. Electing John Kinsey in the place of their recusant speaker, they presently expelled Coxe, and the other absentees, for "contempt of authority, and neglect of the service of their country." Several of the expelled members were re-elected; but the house would not suffer them to take their seats.

During the remainder of his administration, Hunter got along quite smoothly. And when, in 1719, his health failing, he sought a change of climate, by applying for the government of Jamaica, the two assemblies of New York and New Jersey, in legislative addresses, presented him the warmest testimonials of their esteem and regard. The name of Hunterdon county still bears evidence to the popularity which he obtained.

The honest and amiable William Burnet, son of the celebrated Bishop, was presently commissioned as governor of the two provinces.

Enrolling Morris among the number of his intimates, and exercising those popular qualities he possessed in an eminent degree, he easily overcame the slight opposition of his first New Jersey assembly. In return for his ready assent to a scheme for increasing the circulating medium of the province, they granted him an annual salary of five hundred pounds for five years.

After a quiet and harmonious administration of nearly seven years, Burnet's enemies in New York procured his removal, greatly to his own and to the assembly's regret. As a compensation in some sort, the government of Massachusetts Bay was conferred upon him. Departing unwillingly to Boston, he remained there until his sudden death, in the fall of 1729.

The successor of Burnet was John Montgomery, one of the favourites of George II. Of mediocre talents and yielding disposition, the brief period of his administration presents nothing of marked historical importance.

After the death of Montgomery, in 1731, the assembly petitioned for a separate governor. The chief officers of state were either taken from New York, or, upon their appointment, removed thither; and it was there that the governor spent the principal portion of his time. In consequence, the executive and judicial business of the province was subjected to frequent and vexatious delays. The grievance was a heavy one; but the petition for its redress received no present attention. Four years passed turbulently away under the rule of William Crosby, the successor of Montgomery, before the Lords of Trade reported favourably to its prayer, in August, 1736. Pending the king's decision, John Hamilton, son of the old proprietor, performed the duties of the executive. At length the request for a separate governor was granted, and, in 1738, Morris, the favourite of the people, received the royal commission.

Great rejoicings greeted the accession of Morris, and he entered upon his duties under the most flattering auspices. In replying to his address, the assembly expressed the most sanguine expectations of his administration. Appropriating five hundred pounds as a compensation for his services in procuring the late separation, they cheerfully voted him an annual salary of one thousand pounds for three years.

But this clear prospect was soon clouded. Estimating his own abilities highly, ambitious, and tenacious of power, Morris, with the testiness of advanced age, became entangled in repeated quarrels with his assemblies, and finally found himself as odious as he had once been popular. Declaring that the desire common to all the colonies, of rendering the executive dependent on the people, "was nowhere pursued with more steadiness or less decency than in New Jersey," he in turn displayed an obstinate zeal in upholding the prerogative of the crown, entirely unexpected from one who had formerly been the popular champion against it. He proposed no arbitrary or unjust enactment, but caused the defeat of many that would have benefitted the province. Worrying the assembly with frequent prorogations, adjournments, and dissolutions, he rendered himself the most obnoxious of the royal governors, Cornbury only excepted.

In 1744, the peace between England and France was again ruptured. The contest that ensued soon extended to the colonies. Having planned the capture of Louisburg, Shirley, of Massachusetts, invited the other provinces to co-operate. The assembly of New Jersey, then engaged in a sharp controversy with Morris, had refused to organize the militia, or to vote supplies, unless the governor would first consent to sanction some of their cherished measures. The chief of these were an act ordering a new issue of paper money; an act to compel sheriffs to give security for the faithful discharge of their duties; and a bill to prevent actions for small sums in the supreme court. Though loudly called for by the people, these laws were calculated to lessen the power and influence of the executive.

Morris would not yield, while the assembly prepared to starve him into acquiescence, by refusing to grant his salary. They furnished, however, two thousand pounds toward the Louisburg expedition, which was abundantly successful; but they would not order a levy.

Morris stubbornly held out against the assembly, and the vexatious dispute was maintained with much bitterness, until cut short by the death of the governor, on the 21st of May, 1746. His name, borne by one of the counties of the state, still testifies to the early popularity of one whose widow applied vainly to the assembly for the arrears due on her husband's salary.

After the death of Morris, the government devolved upon Hamilton, as president of the council.

Encouraged by the reduction of Louisburg, the colonies were led to entertain their old project of conquering Canada. For this purpose, the New Jersey assembly readily sanctioned a levy of five hundred troops. In less than two months, over six hundred zealous colonists were ready for the field. Formed into five companies, under the command of Colonel Peter Schuyler, they presently marched to the rendezvous at Albany. But the energy of the provinces was weakly seconded by the home government. Neither general, troops, nor orders, came from England, and the enterprise was finally abandoned.

By both parties hostilities were feebly maintained, until brought to a close by the peace of Aix-la-Chapelle, in 1748. To the intense mortification of the colonists, Cape Breton, and Louisburg its capital, so dearly bought by provinçial blood and treasure, were restored to the French almost without an equivalent.

CHAPTER X.

Belcher governor—Revival of quit-rent disputes—A commission of inquiry ordered by the crown—Claims of France to the Ohio valley—Mission of George Washington to Fort Le Bœuf—The works commenced at the forks of the Ohio seized by the French—Washington ordered to protect the Virginia frontier—Skirmish and death of Jumonville—Formal declaration of war—A plan of colonial confederation proposed—Rejected by the provinces and the Board of Trade—Campaign of 1755—Defeat of Braddock—Victory of Lake George—Alarm of the colonies—Indian incursions—Campaign of 1756—Loudoun appointed commander-in-chief—Descent of Montcalm on the forts at Oswego—Treaty with the Delawares.

SHORTLY after the death of Hamilton, in 1747, Jonathan Belcher, previously of Massachusetts, received the royal appointment as governor of New Jersey. Adopting a conciliatory policy with regard to the paper-currency bill, and other popular measures, he was enabled to maintain a tolerably fair understanding with the assembly, though at the expense of a rebuke from the Lords of Trade.

But the ten years of his administration was not undisturbed. In the time of Morris, the old quit-rent dispute, one of the most vexatious that could agitate the province, had been revived with unusual asperity.

Large tracts of the proprietary lands had fallen into the possession of influential persons, fully disposed to urge their titles against those contended for by the Elizabethtown claimants, under the sanction of Indian conveyances. By the former, writs of ejectment were issued, and suits for the recovery of quit-rents commenced against their opponents. The latter resisted violently, and, in 1748, associating themselves for mutual protection, they broke open the jail of Essex county, and liberated a person imprisoned at the suit of the proprietors. Long after the death of Morris, their combination enabled them to defy the civil authorities, and the sympathies of the popular branch of the assembly prevented a military interference.

When Belcher took charge of the province, this trouble was at its height. An assembly being summoned, efforts were made to heal the disorders. The task was one of difficulty. Applying to the king, the governor, and the council, each party sought to criminate the other. The proprietors petitioned that it should be made felony for twelve or more persons to remain assembled, after having been commanded to disperse by the civil authorities. But the popular branch of the assembly refused to legislate against the resistants. A subsequent act, promising pardon and oblivion of offences upon certain conditions, met with no hearty response from them, while the proprietors complained that it was calculated rather to encourage than to intimidate the rioters.

In 1751 a commission of inquiry was ordered from England. In the mean time the Elizabethtown claimants clung to their possessions, thus obtaining what they deemed equal to a victory. But for many years the province was disturbed by dissensions springing from this fruitful source. During the whole period of Belcher's administration, it was seldom that the house and the council could be brought to agree, even upon matters disconnected with it; while, up to the time of the Revolution, a chancery suit, now begun by the proprietors against the Elizabethtown claimants, remained pending without any decision.

Hostilities between France and England soon involved again the colonies. At the best but a hollow truce, the Treaty of Aix-la-Chapelle was early disregarded. Only two years after its conclusion, both nations, taking advantage of the undetermined condition of their territorial limits, began to adopt active and systematic measures for increasing their possessions as much as possible.

To uphold their claims to the country on the Ohio, the French, far more energetic than their English rivals, erected forts Le Bœuf and Venango, the one on French Creek, and the other on the main stream of the Alleghany. Claiming this territory for Great Britain, Dinwiddie of Virginia despatched George Washington, then a young militia officer and a surveyor by profession, to inquire into the designs of the French. Washington was treated with studied courtesy by the commandant at Le Bœuf, but obtained no official satisfaction with regard to the object of his mission. Heated with wine, the French officers, however, made no secret of the intention of France to secure possession of the entire region on the Ohio and the lakes.

Authorized to repel such aggression by force, Dinwiddie presently sent a captain's command to build a fort at the confluence of the Alleghany and Monongahela. Some time in April, 1754, this party was driven off by the French, who took possession of the unfinished works, completed them, and named the fortification Duquesne.

Washington was immediately despatched to protect the frontier thus invaded. Temporarily successful over the enemy under Jumonville, he was subsequently compelled to surrender, after a brief but spirited resistance, and on favourable conditions, to a greatly superior force of French and Indians.

These occurrences gave the signal for hostilities, though war was not formally proclaimed until 1756. Under the circumstances, a union of the colonies was deemed desirable. A plan for such a union, drawn up by Franklin, was adopted by a convention of committees from several colonial assemblies, which met at Albany, in June, 1754. By this plan, a grand council of representatives from the colonial assemblies, presided over by a governor-general appointed by the crown, were to enact general laws, and provide for the common defence of the colonies. Containing germs of the present federal compact, it can scarcely be claimed as original with Franklin. So early as 1722, Coxe, the expelled speaker of the New Jersey house, had proposed a plan resembling it closely.

Submitted to the Lords of Trade, and to the provincial assemblies, Franklin's scheme was rejected by the former, as being too favourable to colonial independence, and by the latter as giving undue power to the crown. The New Jersey assembly, which had declined sending commissioners to the convention, voted against the proposition, because "it might be prejudicial to the prerogative, *and* to the liberties of the people."

Probably the most powerful motive for the rejection of this plan, by the Board of Trade, originated in their desire to secure the adoption of one of their own. In the scheme they had already suggested, taxation of the provinces by parliamentary enactment was advocated. Nothing could have been more hateful to the colonists. The ministerial project was dropped without the formality of a distinct rejection.

Finding war inevitable, the English government appointed General Braddock commander-in-chief of the army in North America. Early in 1755 he was despatched with two regiments to the colonies. Anticipating his arrival, the several provincial assemblies were called upon for troops. The summons was willingly responded to. New Jersey ordered the levy of a regiment five hundred strong, the command of which was given to the veteran Schuyler. Seventy thousand pounds of new paper were issued to pay the expenses of these troops.

Arriving early in March, Braddock met a council of colonial governors at Alexandria, on the Potomac, to concert measures for a campaign. Separate but simultaneous expeditions were planned against Niagara, Crown Point, and Fort Duquesne.

Apprehending most an invasion through New York from Canada, the two northern expeditions were especially favoured by New Jersey. Having been provided with arms from Virginia, at the expense of the assembly, Schuyler's regiment proceeded to the rendezvous at Albany, while Braddock was pursuing his slow and toilsome march to the forks of the Ohio. At Albany, the regiment appears to have been divided; part being joined to the Crown Point expedition, under Colonel Johnson, of New York, while Schuyler, with the remainder, accompanied Shirley, the governor of Massachusetts, in his march to attack Niagara.

Leading the advance against Crown Point, Lyman, of Connecticut, by the 8th of August, had completed Fort Edward, at the portage between the Hudson and Lake George. Johnson presently came up, and marched the main army to the southern shore of the lake, where a strong camp was formed.

Meanwhile the Baron Dieskau, with four thousand French troops, had arrived in Canada. Hearing that Johnson contemplated an attack on Crown Point, Dieskau sought to divert his attention, by advancing upon Fort Edward, at the head of a mixed force of regulars, Canadians and savages.

Tidings of the French general's movement having reached the English camp, Johnson sent forward a detachment of one thousand provincials to relieve the fort. Dieskau, however, had changed his mind, and was advancing upon Johnson himself. Ignorant of this, the detachment marched without caution, unapprehensive of meeting the enemy. Suddenly, when about three miles from the camp, they encountered the whole force of the French. A fierce and sanguinary conflict ensued. Fighting gallantly against superior numbers, the provincials fell back slowly toward the camp, with the loss of their commander, Colonel Williams.

Pressing the fugitives, Dieskau hoped to penetrate the camp, in the midst of the confusion it was expected that their appearance would create. But Johnson was prepared. A few pieces of cannon, hastily brought from the lake shore, opened upon the French as they came in sight. The Indians and Canadians took to the woods, leaving Dieskau, with his regulars alone, to break the English lines. Struggling obstinately for victory, the gallant regulars, during five hours, rushed again and again, only to be repulsed, upon the slight breastwork of the Americans. At length they faltered. Springing from behind their entrenchments, the provincials drove them back in disorder. Thrice wounded, the brave but unfortunate Dieskau, was unable to follow his vanquished army. Seated upon the stump of a tree, with his military trappings by his side, he was found by a renegade Frenchman, fired at, and wounded fatally.

The battle of Lake George was celebrated as a triumph; but Johnson neglected, or was unable to improve his success. Crown Point was left untried, and the French were permitted to fortify themselves at Ticonderoga. During the fall, however, the provincials were employed in building Fort William Henry. Garrisoning the new fortress with six hundred men, Johnson dismissed the remainder to their homes.

Meanwhile, Shirley had performed a slow and toilsome march to Oswego, reaching that place during the month of August. In the midst of extensive preparations for embarking to the siege of Niagara, most discouraging news arrived from Braddock, with whom the expedition was to co-operate. That brave, but vain-glorious and self-opinionated commander, disregarding the wholesome advice of his provincial officers, had met disastrous defeat and death while on his way to besiege Fort Duquesne. Disheartened by this intelligence, and delayed by heavy rains, Shirley finally abandoned his design against Niagara. In the mean time, two substantial forts had been built upon the right and left banks of the Oswego River, a short distance from the lake. Leaving in these strong garrisons, including the New Jersey troops under Schuyler, Shirley returned to Albany.

Braddock's defeat filled the colonies with alarm. The whole western frontier was left exposed to the horrors of savage warfare. Belcher immediately summoned an assembly, but nearly six months elapsed before they awoke to the full necessity of answering the call. Meanwhile the hitherto faithful Delawares were swept away in the general Indian defection. Inflicting the most terrible cruelties, numerous bands of savages roamed without molestation along the western lines of Virginia and Pennsylvania, and finally crossed the Delaware into New Jersey.

In this emergency, the zeal of the inhabitants of Sussex county was displayed. To the number of four hundred, they marched promptly to Easton, under the command of Colonel John Anderson. Their presence was of great service in overawing the Indian bands. Aged and infirm, Belcher was yet active in calling out the resources of the province. When the assembly met in December, Schuyler and his half regiment were recalled from Oswego. Stationed on the frontier, they remained there until the opening of spring, when they again marched to the north, their place being supplied by volunteers.

During the winter, however, outlying parties

of the savages hung around the settlements, rendering it necessary to erect numerous forts and blockhouses, among the mountains and along the Delaware. But the actual hurt they wrought was far less than the intense apprehension their vicinity excited.

Neglected success, failure, and deplorable defeat, had distinguished the campaign of 1755. That of 1756 was altogether disastrous. Elevated by the death of Braddock to the chief command, Shirley, on the opening of spring, began extensive preparations for important expeditions to the north. His exertions had assembled a considerable force at Albany, when he was notified to return to England.

A procrastinater by habit, Lord Loudoun, the successor of Shirley, did not arrive until the summer was well-nigh spent. While General Webb, with a regiment of regulars, was to reinforce Oswego, Loudoun determined to proceed with the main army against Crown Point and Ticonderoga. Great expense had been incurred by the northern colonies, and it was still hoped that the campaign would result in a success proportioned to the outlay. But this expectation was doomed to disappointment.

Having succeeded Dieskau as commander of the French forces in Canada, the Marquis of Montcalm, at the head of five thousand regulars, militia, and Indians, suddenly appeared before the forts at Oswego, on the evening of the twelfth of August. Against Fort Ontario, crowning an eminence opposite to, and commanding the main works, Montcalm opened a heavy cannonade early in the following morning. Gallantly sustaining this during the day, the besieged, finding their ammunition expended, at nightfall spiked their cannon and silently crossed to Oswego. The deserted post was immediately occupied by Montcalm. On the fourteenth, Mercer the English commander was slain. After a brief bombardment, the disheartened garrison surrendered as prisoners of war. Few perished on either side, but the French were overjoyed with the amount of their booty. Six ships of war, three hundred boats, immense stores of ammunition and provisions, one hundred and twenty cannon and sixteen hundred troops fell thus easily into their hands. To allay the jealousy of his savage allies, the politic Montcalm destroyed both forts and left Oswego a solitude.

Tardily advancing, Webb met the disastrous tidings at the Oneida portage. He fell back with precipitation to Albany. Disconcerted by these events, Loudoun recalled the troops marching against Ticonderoga, dismissed the provincials, and abandoned all offensive operations for the campaign.

Among the prisoners at Oswego, were Schuyler and his half regiment. Carried to Canada, a new enlistment presently supplied their loss. Schuyler, however, was soon released on parole, with the promise that he would return if no suitable exchange should be offered for him. Welcomed home with illuminations and other tokens of joy, the veteran colonel remained there until the spring of 1758. It was then that the French commandant in Canada "sent to demand the brave old Peter Schuyler of New Jersey, as no person had been exchanged for him." Thrusting aside the friends who entreated him to stay, the gallant old officer, true to his plighted word, went back again into captivity.

Meanwhile, Sir William Johnson had succeeded in procuring at Easton a treaty of peace with the Delawares. A partial relief was thus afforded to the western frontiers. But during the spring and summer of 1757, a continual alarm was kept up by scalping parties of savages from Canada and the Ohio. Committing depredations within thirty miles of Philadelphia, these bands did not neglect to visit the north-western settlements of New Jersey, for the protection of which it was found necessary to maintain a company of Rangers.

CHAPTER XI.

Increase of British power in the colonies—Subordination of colonial officers—Indignation in Pennsylvania and New Jersey—Campaign of 1757—Co-operation of New Jersey—Expedition against Louisburg—Inactivity of Loudoun at Halifax—Energetic movements of Montcalm—Siege of Fort William Henry—Surrender of Munro—Attempted massacre of the prisoners—Heroic conduct of Montcalm—Alarm of General Webb—Death of Governor Belcher—Campaign of 1758—Masterly arrangements of Pitt—Hearty response of the colonies—Capture of Louisburg—Repulse of Abercrombie before Ticonderoga—Fort Frontenac taken by Bradstreet—Evacuation of Fort Duquesne—Indian council at the forks of the Delaware—Campaign of 1759—Invasion of Canada projected—Ticonderoga and Crown Point abandoned by the French—Surrender of Fort Niagara—Capture of Quebec—Peace of Fontainebleau—Change of governors in New Jersey—Indian outrages.

During the year 1756 Parliament had effected a signal extension of its authority over the colonies. Military rule, enforced with imperious arrogance by Loudoun had been established, independent of the provincial governments. By its power, troops had been quartered upon the inhabitants against their indignant and earnest remonstrances, and the colonial officers had been degraded to a position inferior to that of those commissioned by the crown. The people of Pennsylvania and New Jersey had been irritated by the authority given to recruiting officers, to enlist their indentured servants. Militia companies, assembled for mutual defence against a barbarous foe, had been arbitrarily dismissed; while the intercession of the Quakers with the Delawares, to obtain security for their hearths and cradles in the more peaceful way of interchanging faith and presents, was condemned as a most daring violation of the royal prerogative.

The indignation excited by these measures was intensely aggravated by Loudoun's attributing the disastrous result of the past year's operations, properly due to his own incapacity, to the colonial troops. Still, in preparing for the campaign of 1757, he was well seconded by the colonial assemblies, though not to the extent of his demands. New Jersey would not authorize a conscription to raise her regiment of five hundred to a thousand.

The capture of Louisburg was to be the principal object of the campaign. Leaving the newly-raised levies from New England, New York, and New Jersey, to garrison Forts Edward and William Henry, Loudoun sailed with six thousand regulars for Halifax. Arriving there, he found himself at the head of an excellent army ten thousand strong, supported by a large and effective fleet. August came, and the indecisive chief was still at Halifax, amusing himself with planting cabbages. At length the troops were embarked; but news arrived that the harbour of Louisburg was defended by seventeen ships of the line. Loudoun then sailed for New York. His great preparations had ended in nothing.

Meantime, his energetic and wily opponent, Montcalm, was not idle. Availing himself of Loudoun's unskilfulness in withdrawing so large a portion of the British force from the frontiers of New York, he ascended Lake George with eight thousand men, and laid siege to Fort William Henry. In the fort itself, less than five hundred British regulars were posted under Lieutenant-Colonel Munro. On an eminence to the south-east, the provincials, including the unfortunate New Jersey regiment, were entrenched to the number of seventeen hundred men. On the morning of the fourth of August, the artillery of the French opened. For six days the attack was maintained with daring ardour. But not until the expiration of that period would the gallant Munro capitulate, and then only because half his guns were burst and his ammunition wellnigh expended. The conditions of surrender were, that the English should be suffered to depart with the honours of war, on a pledge not to serve against the French for eighteen months. An escort sufficient to protect them from Montcalm's barbarian allies was to attend their march to Fort Edward, some twelve miles distant.

Montcalm made every effort to fulfil his pledges. But dissatisfied with his clemency, and rendered furious by strong drink, the savages fell upon the English as they filed out of their entrenchments. Without arms, they could make no defence. Twenty, or thereabouts, were tomahawked on the spot. The rest fled; some to the wilderness, others to the French camp. Montcalm and his officers exerted themselves daringly to stay the slaughter. "Kill me!" cried the mortified general; "Kill me, but spare the English, who are under my protection." In the flight to Fort Edward, a few more were slain or made prisoners by the savages. Six hundred reached there in a body; many stragglers followed; and four hundred afterward came in under a strong escort of French troops.

All this time Webb was at Fort Edward, with six thousand men under his command, and a numerous militia within call. Yet he remained inactive, not daring to sally from his stronghold. Roused at length by his personal fears, he summoned assistance. His call was answered promptly. From New Jersey alone a thousand militia hastened toward his camp, while three thousand more were ready to march if it should be necessary. But it was now too late. Satisfied with the triumph he had achieved, Montcalm retreated to Canada. Thus disastrously for the English terminated the campaign of 1757.

Meanwhile Governor Belcher had died, worn out with years, and not unregretted. The executive duties now devolved for a brief period upon the president of the council, the aged John Reading.

With the opening of the campaign of 1758 a brighter prospect dawned upon the dejected and mortified colonists. William Pitt, the elder, was now at the head of the British cabinet. Uniting the same energy and steadfastness to well-formed aims, that had elevated him from a cornetcy in the dragoons to his present lofty station, he determined upon overthrowing the Gallic dominion in North America. In his preparations he exhibited a full and just knowledge of the temper and disposition of the colonists. The obnoxious Loudoun was recalled. The galled sense of honour of the provincial officers was soothed by allowing all, from the rank of colonel downward, an equal command with the British. A powerful fleet and army were despatched to America. To co-operate with these forces, the several colonies were invited to raise such a number of levies as their circumstances would permit. Arms, ammunition, tents, and provisions were to be furnished by the crown. The provinces were to pay and clothe their levies, but for these expenses even, Pitt promised to endeavour to procure a parliamentary reimbursement.

The effect was magical. Instead of reluctantly raising five hundred levies, the New Jersey assembly, offering a bounty of twelve pounds to each recruit, called for a thousand, and voted fifty thousand pounds for their support. Bar racks, each capable of accommodating three hundred men, were ordered to be built at Burlington, Trenton, New Brunswick, Amboy, and Elizabethtown. Nor was a less energetic spirit exhibited by the other colonies. Nearly thirty thousand provincials took up arms. With these and the regulars, Abercrombie, the new commander-in-chief, found himself at the head of fifty thousand effective troops.

Three several expeditions were set in motion; Abercrombie against Ticonderoga and Crown Point; Forbes against Duquesne; and Amherst and Wolfe, in conjunction with Boscawen's fleet, against Louisburg.

Amherst was the first to move. Appearing before Louisburg on the 6th of June, he immediately began a vigorous siege. After an obstinate defence of seven weeks, in which they suffered severe loss, the garrison, three thousand strong, surrendered as prisoners of war. The whole country around the Gulf of St. Lawrence thus fell into the power of the English.

Meanwhile, Abercrombie had assembled on the margin of Lake George an army of sixteen thousand men, seven thousand being British regulars, and the remainder provincials from New England, New York, and New Jersey. At early dawn on July the fifth, they embarked on more than a thousand boats, and to the stirring tones of martial music, with bright banners and gay uniforms gleaming in the morning sun, moved swiftly down the lake to attack Ticonderoga. Landing near the outlet of the lake, at nine o'clock the next day, they began their march, over a rough road, and led by bewildered guides. Some confusion took place in the van, during which a scouting party of the French was encountered. The loss of the English was trifling in point of numbers, but among the slain was young Lord Howe, the moving spirit of the army.

Passing the night in the wilderness, Abercrombie returned to the landing-place, and took a new and shorter route, which the energy of Bradstreet, an active provincial officer, had opened to within a mile and a half of the French works. Too impatient to wait for his artillery, he rashly ordered an assault on the front of the enemy's line.

Ticonderoga was held by about thirty-four hundred men, under the command of the watchful and sagacious Montcalm. Early informed of the approach of the English, he had with wonderful activity wellnigh completed his defences before they made their appearance. The most formidable portion of his works was that which Abercrombie had determined to storm. It consisted of a breast-work nine feet high, built of huge logs, and guarded in front by felled trees, with their branches sharpened, and pointing outward like lances. Behind this Montcalm posted his troops, with orders not to fire a gun until the storming party should become entangled among the stumps and rubbish of all sorts, by which their advance was impeded.

Having formed in three columns, the British regulars rushed gallantly to the assault. Commanded to reserve their fire until the breast-work should be carried, they were struggling over the encumbered ground in front, when a deadly and incessant discharge broke from the French lines. Though thrown at once into confusion, they fought bravely and long. For four hours they endeavoured with heroic obstinacy, but in vain, to execute the ill-timed and injudicious orders of their chief. Finally, having lost over two thousand in killed and wounded, they abandoned the hopeless contest. On the next morning Abercrombie conducted a hasty and confused retreat to Fort William Henry.

To balance this ill fortune, in part at least, the energetic Bradstreet presently projected the surprise of Frontenac, a fortress on the Canadian shore of Lake Ontario. His success was signal. An immense amount of valuable stores, nine armed vessels, and the command of the lake thus fell into the hands of the English.

The destruction of Frontenac contributed largely to the success of the western expedition under Forbes. Deprived by that event of their wonted supplies, the garrison at Fort Duquesne, upon the approach of the English, set fire to their works and fled precipitately down the Ohio. The charred ruins were yet smoking when Washington with the vanguard of the army took possession of the deserted post.

Meanwhile, the triumphs of the campaign had been enhancéd by the restoration of peace along the western borders. After several preliminary conferences, Bernard, now governor of the province, aided by the good offices of Teedyscung, one of their bravest and most eloquent chiefs, prevailed upon the New Jersey tribes to attend "the grand council-fire, kindled at the forks of the Delaware." Here were met the representatives of the Iroquois and their subject tribes, to treat with the commissioners of Pennsylvania and New Jersey. "We now take the hatchet out of your hands," said the red man solemnly to the commissioners. "It was a French hatchet. We take it out of your hands and bury it in the ground, where it shall rest for ever."

Many strings of wampum confirmed the truth of their words, and the broken chain of friendship was re-united with strong links.

At a subsequent special conference, the New Jersey tribes sold all their remaining lands to the province. The Delawares presently emigrated to the country west of the Alleghanies, while the Minnisinks, numbering about one hundred and fifty souls, authorized the purchase of three thousand acres, on the eastern shore of Burlington county, where they were removed at the expense of the colony. Here, in possession of fine hunting grounds and convenient fisheries, they remained quietly for many years, under the protection of special commissioners.

For the campaign of 1759, Pitt planned the conquest of Canada; the young and gallant Wolfe being directed to advance against Quebec, Amherst to take Ticonderoga and Crown Point, and then besiege Montreal; and a third army, composed principally of provincials under Prideaux, to capture Niagara. Of this plan the colonial assemblies were informed under an oath of secrecy. Pitt gained their willing co-operation by a prompt parliamentary reimbursal of the last year's expenses. By spring twenty thousand provincials were in the field. With less than fifteen thousand fighting men, New Jersey raised a thousand troops in addition to the thousand she had already lost. Her expenditures for their support amounted to almost five dollars for every soul in the province.

Pitt's plan for the campaign was but partially accomplished. Amherst, indeed, obtained easy possession of Ticonderoga and Crown Point, but he moved with such dilatory caution that winter put an effectual stop to his operations, while he was yet lingering at the head of Lake Champlain. Prideaux landed successfully before Niagara, but was soon afterward killed by the bursting of a cohorn. Sir William Johnson succeeded to the chief command. Twelve hundred French regulars, hastening to relieve the beleaguered fortress, were signally routed; and finally, after sustaining a siege of nearly three weeks, the garrison, six hundred strong, surrendered as prisoners of war. Destitute of shipping and short of provisions, Johnson was likewise unable to effect the proposed junction with Wolfe on the St. Lawrence. The latter general, however, one of the best and bravest in the British army, with the loss of his life, gained an imperishable renown by winning the most important battle that had ever been fought in the New World. Sailing from Louisburg with eight thousand troops, he landed a short distance below Quebec, on the twenty fifth of June. Nearly three months were spent in unavailing attempts to baffle the watchfulness of the alert Montcalm. But at length, having secretly scaled the Heights of Abraham, Wolfe drew up five thousand of his troops in battle array on the plain before Quebec. Montcalm hastened to meet him, and a sanguinary battle ensued. Wounded twice, Wolfe lived to learn that the French had fled, but no longer. His brave opponent, Montcalm, also received a death-wound in the fight, but did not survive to witness the capitulation of the city, an event which took place five days after the battle.

With Quebec fell the power of France in America. In the following year Montreal was surrendered to the united armies under Amherst; but peace between England and France was for a time deferred, by the "family compact" entered into by the latter country and Spain. The allied powers, however, dispirited by continued defeat, were at length brought to terms, and peace was finally restored by the Treaty of Fontainebleau, on the third of November, 1763. Nova Scotia, Canada and its dependencies, together with the entire command of the country east of the Mississippi, were thus secured to Great Britain.

Meantime, Bernard having been elevated to the government of Massachusetts, transferred that of New Jersey to Thomas Boone. Being presently sent to South Carolina, Boone was succeeded by Josiah Hardy. In 1763, William, the natural and only son of Benjamin Franklin, through the powerful recommendation of Lord Bute, was appointed governor of New Jersey, Hardy having been previously nominated as consul at Cadiz.

Soon after the commencement of Franklin's administration, an extensive conspiracy, having for its object the extermination of the whites, was formed by the Indians of Pennsylvania and of the territory north-west of the Ohio. At the head of the conspiracy of red men was Pontiac, the brave, active, and far-seeing chief of the Ottawas. The frontier posts were attacked and many of them captured. Scalping parties committed their customary atrocities in the border settlements. On the approach of the marauding parties to the western frontier of New Jersey, Governor Franklin extended the line of fortifications and ordered out the militia. But these were insufficient; the savages presently breaking through the line, and cruelly massacreing a number of families. Provision was immediately made by the assembly for the further protection of the frontier, and troops raised to serve with the northern army against the Indians. New Jersey, however, was not again molested.

CHAPTER XII.

Colonial expenditures during the war—Project to tax America—Obnoxious to the colonists—Unanimity of the provinces—Stamp Act proposed—Remonstrance of the colonies—Stamp Act passed—Spirited resolutions of Virginia—National Congress recommended—Disapproved of by the New Jersey house—Indignation of the people against their representatives—House again convenes at Amboy—Delegates appointed to the Congress—Petition and remonstrance forwarded to England—New Jersey stamp-distributor resigns—Stamp Tax repealed—Party lines drawn—Opposition to the Quartering Act—Townsend's tax bill passed—Agitation in the colonies—Language of the New Jersey house—Non-importation agreements—Violated by New York traders—Their reception in New Jersey—Repeal of all taxes except the duty on tea—Popular tumults in Monmouth and Essex counties—Odious nature of the tax on tea—Rendered nugatory by non-importation agreements—Parliament endeavours to force tea into America—Tea destroyed at Boston and in New Jersey—Port of Boston closed—New Jersey people sympathize with their Massachusetts brethren—National Congress of 1774—Battle of Lexington.

IN the long contest but lately terminated, the assistance England had received from her colonies was important. More than thirteen thousand provincials had perished by the sword and the diseases of camps; and more than three millions of pounds were expended by the different colonies. During nearly the whole period of hostilities, New Jersey alone had maintained a thousand troops in the field, at an outlay amounting to over three hundred thousand pounds. Of all the money thus furnished, scarcely one-third had been reimbursed by Parliament.

The promptitude with which the provinces had advanced means, and the little apparent inconvenience they suffered from the large demands made upon them, created in the minds of the English ministers an exaggerated opinion with regard to the wealth and resources of the colonists. England herself had expended immense sums in prosecuting the war. Some portion of this outlay was properly chargeable to the American colonies, and to them, therefore, the ministry were early led to look for réimbursal. With this pretext they immediately prepared to execute a design, conceived indeed long before, but which the necessity of a good feeling on the part of the colonists had hitherto prevented from being prominently brought forward. This was to impose upon them a tax for revenue, thus at once opening a source of emolument and asserting the prerogative of the crown.

Yet the execution of this design was fraught with danger, which, however, but few foresaw. Individually the colonies had on all previous occasions expressed their abhorrence of measures involving the principle of unrepresented taxation. During the late war, the clashing interests that had hitherto divided them were in some degree harmonized. The idea of union in a common cause had become familiar. Nothing could have been better calculated to strengthen that idea than an undue assertion of the royal prerogative. Nor were the colonists illy prepared to resist that assertion. They had become accustomed to arms, and to the discipline of the camp and the field; and by their recent intercourse with one another they had gained a knowledge, hitherto unknown, of their mutual resources and capabilities in the emergency of war.

Notwithstanding the quiet yet pertinacious resistance of the colonies, Parliament had in various ways wielded a sort of power over them, highly obnoxious to some, and greatly detrimental to the interests of all. That which was the most odious—the levying of taxes for revenue—though frequently claimed, had never been exercised. Urged on by Grenville, the English chancellor, Parliament prepared to vindicate its asserted claim. After the adoption of several offensive measures, the House of Commons, in March, 1764, resolved that "it might be proper to charge certain stamp duties in the colonies." In accordance with this resolve a bill was counselled, imposing a duty on stamps, by which various legal and other papers, to be valid in courts of law, were to be drawn up on stamped paper, sold by public officers appointed for that purpose, and at prices which levied a stated tax on every such document.

In America every effort was exerted to prevent the passage of this proposed act; but remonstrances, petitions, and denunciations were equally unavailing. On the twenty-second of March, 1765, it was passed with slight opposition by the Commons, and by the Lords without a division. At the same time an act called the Quartering Act was passed, authorizing the ministry to maintain a standing army in America, the several provincial assemblies being directed to supply the troops with quarters, fuel, lights, drink, soap and bedding.

On receiving intelligence of the passage of these acts, the colonies became agitated by the keenest indignation. With singular unanimity they took bold and determined steps to prevent their effective operation. Virginia was the first to move. By the house of burgesses of that province resolutions were adopted, reciting in the most spirited language the rights and grievances of the colonists. Massachusetts followed, and recommended a National Congress, to meet at New York on the first Tuesday of October.

On the twenty-ninth of June this recommendation was laid before the New Jersey assembly. Few in number, on the point of adjournment, and influenced probably by Franklin, who was an ardent supporter of the prerogative, the house paid but little attention to it, and somewhat hastily signified their disapproval of the proposed convention. Their conduct, however, was keenly censured. So strong was the popular indignation, that Ogden, their speaker, found it necessary, in order to preserve the peace of the province, to convene the members, by circular, at Amboy. In defiance of Franklin's denunciation of their proceedings as "unprecedented, irregular, and unconstitutional," they accordingly met and appointed Joseph Ogden, Hendrick Fisher, and Joseph Borden to be delegates to the National Congress.

At the time and place appointed, delegates from nine provinces assembled, and presently adopted a declaration of rights, in which it was forcibly contended that the colonies could not be taxed unless by their own consent. Eloquent memorials to both Houses of Parliament, and a petition to the king, spirited but respectful, were next agreed to and signed by most of the delegates present. To these, however, Ogden of New Jersey, and Ruggles of Massachusetts, refused to attach their signatures, on the ground that the approval of the several assemblies was first necessary. Ogden's conduct was severely censured at home. He was burned in effigy by the people, and finally forced to resign his place as speaker of the house.

The proceedings of the National Congress were approved without a dissenting voice, by the assembly of New Jersey, which met early in the following month. Reiterating the sentiments adopted in the convention, the house protested strongly against the late Act of Parliament as utterly subversive of their ancient privileges. For this they were sharply reprehended by the governor, and immediately prorogued.

Meanwhile steps of a less legitimate character had been taken to resist the operation of the Stamp Act. Associations designed to unite the people in forcible opposition to it, springing up in New York and Connecticut, and calling themselves the "Sons of Liberty," had extended rapidly into the adjoining colonies. Riots became frequent and alarming. Many of the stamp-officers were frightened into resignation. Others, among whom was Coxe of New Jersey, voluntarily threw up their commissions. And when, on the first of November, the act went into operation, neither stamps nor stamp-officers could be found. The obnoxious measure was in effect nullified.

A change having meanwhile taken place in the British ministry, the colonists were encouraged to maintain their bold and determined stand. Besides, their agreement to import no more

British goods until the Stamp Act should be repealed, began to be felt seriously by the trading interest of England, which was thus led to favour their cause. The eloquence and zeal of Pitt were also exerted in their behalf. Finally, with a show of liberality, but in reality as a matter of expediency, the new ministry procured the repeal of the odious act, in March, 1766. But in order to soothe the irritation of its friends, a bill was previously passed, asserting the power and right of Parliament "to bind the colonies in all cases whatsoever." This, however, was disregarded by the colonists in the joy they experienced at their signal victory.

To the New Jersey assembly, which presently met, Governor Franklin offered his congratulation on the repeal of the Stamp Act. This elicited a cutting reply. Franklin's strenuous efforts to prevent that desirable event were not forgotten. Still the assembly were willing to be grateful to the king and to Parliament for having relieved them from the burden of an "impolitic law."

While with the mass of the colonists satisfaction was the prominent feeling, there were not wanting occasions for angry discussion in regard to the respective rights of the crown and the colonial assemblies. Party lines began to be strongly drawn; such as advocated the royal prerogative being known as Tories, while the opponents of parliamentary taxation received the name of Whigs.

Among other causes for the discontent which soon manifested itself was the enforcing of the Quartering Act. Partially complied with in Massachusetts, in New York it was wholly disregarded. In New Jersey a full compliance with its provisions was refused by the house, who declared that they considered it as much an act for levying taxes as the one recently repealed.

Rockingham's ministry was speedily overturned. With the formation of the new cabinet the aspect of colonial affairs became still more clouded. Charles Townsend, a man of brilliant talents, but with no fixed principle of action, occupied the post of chancellor of the exchequer. Exasperated by the taunts of Grenville, he rashly declared in the House of Commons that he dared to tax America, and forthwith introduced a new scheme for drawing a revenue from the colonies, by a bill imposing custom-house taxation on glass, paper, paints, and tea. With scarcely a show of opposition, the bill was carried through Parliament, in June, 1767.

Justly viewing this measure as identical in principle with the Stamp Act, the colonists at once began to agitate against it; pouring in upon the ministry a continuous stream of petitions and remonstrances, and by essays and legislative resolves expressing the deep conviction that their liberties had been invaded. Though couched in less fiery language than on the previous occasion, these documents were characterized by logical acumen, a clear sense of the rights of the colonies, and a calm but fixed determination to resist all and every attempt at parliamentary taxation.

"Freemen cannot be taxed but by themselves or by their representatives," was the declaration of the New Jersey house of assembly to the king. "This privilege we esteem so invaluable that we are fully persuaded no other can exist without it. Duties have lately been imposed upon us for the sole and express purpose of raising a revenue. Yet, that we are represented in Parliament we not only cannot allow, but are convinced from our local circumstances we never can be."

More effective steps were presently taken. The former non-importation agreements were renewed. As the direct imports of New Jersey were light, she could do little in the matter but encourage her commercial neighbours. At one time a few of the New York traders were induced to violate their voluntary pledges. Some of these persons soon after visiting New Brunswick and Woodbridge to dispose of their goods, the indignant populace fell upon them and drove them with violence from their respective towns. At other places public meetings were held, at which the recusants were held up to the scorn of all true friends of liberty, and bitterly denounced as foul traitors to their country.

At length, as on the previous occasion, the manufacturers and traders of England began to suffer. In their troubles they pressed the repeal of Townsend's obnoxious bill. As it had been almost impossible to enforce that act, nothing scarcely in the shape of revenue had accrued from it, while every day the indignation of the colonists was growing in strength and storminess. Consequently, and moved rather by their fears than by a sense of justice, the ministry procured the repeal of the Revenue Act, in April, 1770, reserving, however, a trifling duty on the single article of tea.

Meanwhile local difficulties had sprung up in New Jersey, which at length led to alarming disturbances. The appearance of extraordinary prosperity occasioned by the late war, had been followed by a period of great and general distress. Bankruptcies and suits-at-law became numerous. Debtors were unable to settle their accounts, while the creditor bold enough to prosecute, together with his attorney, was subjected to the ill-will of the debtor and his exasperated friends. Finally the lawyers became particularly obnoxious. Charging the whole legal fraternity with being a band of extortioners, the people of Monmouth county, in January, 1770, assembled at Freehold, where the court was then holding its session, tumultuously entered the court-house, drove the judges from their benches, and thus put a stop to further judicial proceedings. An attempt at a similar design in Essex county was frustrated by the vigilance of the public officers, assisted by the well-disposed citizens. To meet this crisis, a special meeting of the assembly was called. By the adoption of judicious measures, quiet was at length restored, though not until the passage of a law against excessive costs in the recovery of debts under fifty pounds.

For nearly four years after the partial abrogation of the Revenue Act, nothing of marked historical importance occurred in New Jersey. There, as in most of the other colonies, the period was one of political calm. But Parliament, by retaining the duty on tea, seemed to have established by precedent the right to tax America. As it was the assertion of this right alone that had provoked the resistance of the colonists, the continuance of the tea-duty was a measure as insulting as it was weak. Pecuniarily insignificant, it was momentous in a political point of view. Yet, for a time, the colonists were content with a mere modification of their non-importation agreements so as to include tea only. By this means the tax on tea, as an assertion of parliamentary right, was rendered almost unavailing.

Parliament at length determined upon a new attempt to draw a revenue from America by means of the reserved duty on tea. The colonists having steadily refused to import, seventeen millions of pounds of the obnoxious commodity had collected in the East India Company's warehouses. To force a large quantity of this into the provinces might at once relieve the company from its embarrassment, and bring about the ministerial ends. Removing the export duty, and relieving the company of certain existing restraints, arrangements were made for shipping several cargoes of tea to the chief ports of America, where it was expected it would be received willingly, and readily purchased, now that the duty was only a nominal one.

But the colonists were vigilant. From New Hampshire to Georgia the cry of imperilled freedom was again heard. Immediate steps were taken to avert the danger that so insidiously presented itself. In some places the tea was permitted to be landed and stored, but not to be sold. At Boston, when the tea-ships arrived, they were boarded by a party disguised as Indians, and their cargoes cast into the sea. As the vessels were approaching New York and Philadelphia, they were stopped and compelled to return home. At Annapolis, the owner was forced to set fire to the vessel containing the tea. The cargo of a ship landed and stored at Greenwich, New Jersey, late in 1774, was seized upon by the populace, and publicly burned to ashes.

This bold overthrow of their plans goaded the ministry wellnigh to fury. Upon Massachusetts fell the heaviest stroke of their indignation. Stringent acts were hurried through Parliament, directed especially against the people of that province. Among others, bills to shut the port of Boston, and to subvert, in effect, the charter of the colony. The tidings speedily reached America. Sympathizing with Massachusetts, the colonies at once rose in her behalf. With their commerce annihilated by the Port Bill, the people of Boston soon stood in need of assistance. Contributions flowed into them from all parts of the country, and from no province more freely than from New Jersey. Forwarding their first "present," the inhabitants of Monmouth exhorted their Boston brethren "not to give up, and if they should want a further supply of bread to let them know." The people of Elizabethtown were equally liberal, and from Salem one hundred and fifty pounds were sent to "the distressed and suffering poor of Boston."

Matters were now approaching a crisis. Thoroughly aroused by the recent action of the ministry and of Parliament, the colonists prepared for active and determined resistance. A national Congress was recommended, to be composed of delegates from the several provinces. This recommendation met a hearty response from all sides. On the fifth of September, 1774, delegates from twelve colonies convened at Philadelphia, and, after a long and anxious session, adopted a petition to the king, a declaration of rights, a memorial to the people of England, and an address to the inhabitants of Canada.

The proceedings of this Congress were laid before the New Jersey assembly, on the 24th of January, 1775. Notwithstanding the strenuous endeavours of Governor Franklin to prevent it, the house approved of the report unanimously, save that the Quaker members excepted to such portions as seemed to look toward forcible resistance.

From this period the aspect of affairs continued to grow more and more troubled; and at length by the battle of Lexington, on the 19th of April, the War of Independence was fairly opened. Little hope was now left of a peaceful adjustment of the difficulties existing between the colonies and the mother country.

CHAPTER XIII.

Affair of Lexington—Military activity of the provincials—Proceedings of Congress—Ticonderoga surprised by Ethan Allen—Lord North's conciliatory plan rejected by New Jersey—Organization of the militia—Battle of Bunker Hill—Evacuation of Boston by the British—Declaration of Independence—State of New Jersey formed—Livingston elected governor—New York menaced by Howe—Activity of Washington—Battle of Long Island—New York evacuated by the Americans—Capture of Fort Washington by the British—Retreat of Washington across the Jerseys—Condition of his troops—Meeting of the first state legislature—The American army crosses the Delaware—Capture of General Lee—Surprise of the Hessians at Trenton.

THE affair at Lexington kindled a spirit of resolute resistance throughout the country. In New England especially, extraordinary zeal was displayed by the provincials. Within two days after the fight an irregular volunteer force of twenty thousand men had beleaguered Boston. In the middle and southern colonies a spirit scarcely less active and prompt was displayed, and every thing betokened that an earnest and determined struggle was at hand.

To the Continental Congress, which met in May, public attention was anxiously directed. Declaring that hostilities were already begun by Great Britain, they prepared to put the colonies in a posture of defence. As no general idea was yet entertained of independence, a firm but respectful petition to the king was resolved upon, while memorials were addressed to the people of England, Ireland, and Quebec; in which, boldly stating the rights of the colonies, Congress spiritedly vindicated its former course and its present designs.

While the National Congress was thus engaged, a party of provincials, led by Ethan Allen and Seth Warner, had captured the fortresses of Ticonderoga and Crown Point. Artillery, and a large amount of ammunition and military stores thus fell into the hands of the needy colonists.

Five days afterward, on the 15th of May, the New Jersey assembly, at the call of Franklin, convened to consider the specious but unconcessive "conciliatory plan" of Lord North. Though recommended earnestly by the governor in an elaborate address, the house firmly and solemnly declined assenting to the proposition. Finding them immovable, Franklin ordered an adjournment. Subsequently a few days, a Provincial Congress convened at Trenton, and agreed upon an association for the defence of colonial rights against the aggression of the British ministry. Declining to authorize a levy of regular troops until some general plan should be formed, they adopted measures for organizing the militia, and ordered the issue of ten thousand pounds in bills of credit, to defray expenses.

At length the battle of Bunker Hill, on the 17th of June, wellnigh brought all hope of reconciliation to an end. In the mean time, the National Congress had made arrangements for a continental army, at the head of which was George Washington of Virginia. Washington presently took command of the provincials investing Boston. While he was busied in organizing these brave but untrained troops, Congress engaged itself in providing for their support, pay, and government.

On the fifth of August the Provincial Congress of New Jersey again met, and made further provision for organizing the militia, to command which they appointed Philemon Dickinson and William Livingston, both persons already celebrated for their patriotism. Having chosen a provincial treasurer and a committee of safety, the congress adjourned. Meeting again on the third of October, they ordered the enlistment of two regiments of regulars, the command of one of which was given to William Maxwell, and of the other to William Alexander, commonly called Lord Stirling. Thirty thousand pounds were issued in provincial bills, to defray the expenses thus incurred.

Meanwhile Franklin had been active in his opposition. Convening the general assembly on the sixteenth of November, he complained to the members that "sentiments of independence had been openly avowed, and that essays had appeared, ridiculing the people's fears of that horrid measure." In reply, the house declared that they knew "of no sentiments of independency openly avowed," and that they "approved of no essays tending to such a measure." They remained in session, transacting their ordinary business, until the 6th of December, when they were prorogued for a brief period. But they never again met.

To meet a requisition for additional troops, the Provincial Congress assembled at New Brunswick, on the 31st of January, 1776. An attack upon the colonies through Canada having been planned by England, the Continental Congress determined to thwart it by a counter-movement. In this exigency, New Jersey ordered the enlistment of another regiment, and made a further appropriation of twenty thousand pounds.

Meanwhile Washington had maintained a close investment of the British in Boston. Wearied out at length, they evacuated the city in March, when the triumphant provincials took immediate and joyful possession.

For nearly a year the colonists had been in arms against the mother country. Entire independence, however, had not as yet been asserted.

But on the seventh of June, it was at length moved in the National Congress, "that the United Colonies are, and ought to be, free and indepedent states; and that their political connection with Great Britain is, and ought to be, dissolved." The resolution passed by a small majority. The delegates from New Jersey had been expressly instructed against it. Presently, however, a new set was chosen, with directions to cast their suffrages for independence. On the fourth of July following, a formal declaration to that effect was adopted by the Continental Congress, and signed by most of the members present.

Already the Congress of New Jersey had prepared and adopted a new and independent constitution; and, having presently agreed to the national declaration, they assumed the style and title of the "Convention of the State of New Jersey." On the 31st of August following, William Livingston, commander-in-chief of the militia, was elected the first governor of the state—Franklin, the old colonial executive, having been made prisoner some time previously for corresponding with the enemy. Removed to Connecticut, Franklin was there kept in close confinement until the end of the war, when he sailed, a voluntary exile from the country of his birth, to England.

Meanwhile the arms of the provincials had

met with a series of disasters. The campaign against Canada, which opened with the most brilliant prospect of success, had terminated in the precipitate retreat of the American forces to Crown Point, and subsequently to Ticonderoga.

Early in July, General Howe, with the late garrison of Boston, and other troops from Halifax, landed on Staten Island, from which he threatened an attack on the city of New York. Calling upon New York and New Jersey for troops, Washington immediately hastened to defend the beleaguered city. In a month's time, by dint of extraordinary exertions, he was enabled to swell his army to about twenty thousand sickly, ill-equipped, and half-trained soldiers. His opponent, meanwhile, had received numerous reinforcements, raising his force to nearly twenty-four thousand of the best troops in the British service.

At length Howe began to move. Advancing cautiously by the way of Long Island, he succeeded, after subjecting the Americans to a disastrous defeat, in encamping in front of their lines at Brooklyn, on the night of the 27th of August. Washington presently retreated across the East River. Howe followed on the 13th of September, and landed three miles above New York, putting to dastardly flight the provincials stationed to oppose him. The city was immediately abandoned by the Americans, and the British took possession.

Washington intrenched himself on Harlem Heights. After a series of cautious movements on the part of both generals, Howe seemed to threaten New Jersey, when the main body of the Continental army crossed to the west bank of the Hudson, under the immediate direction of Washington himself. On the 16th of November, Fort Washington, with its numerous garrison and immense stores, fell into the enemy's hands. Fort Lee, on the Jersey shore of the Hudson, was hastily evacuated by the Americans. Washington, whose army was now reduced to four thousand men, took ground on a level plain between the Hackensack and Passaic, but a superior British force under Cornwallis advancing against him, he was compelled to commence a rapid retreat across the Jerseys.

This retreat was accompanied by almost every circumstance that could harass and depress the spirits. The severity of winter had already set in. Depressed by a succession of disasters, the little army of Americans moved wearily on, illy clad, without tents, and with scarcely a blanket to protect them from the rigor of the season. Pressing them closely was the force of Cornwallis, flushed with previous good fortune, wanting none of the necessaries of camp, and dazzling by the brilliancy of their equipments. It is scarcely to be wondered, then, that the militia of New Jersey, upon contrasting the different appearance of the two armies, exhibited a reluctance to take the field, though every exertion was made by their new and popular governor to induce them to rally in defence of their country and its liberties.

The first legislature under the lately-formed constitution was still in session at Princeton, when the flying Americans made their appearance. They immediately broke up, to assemble again at Burlington; but the tide of war advancing upon them there, they retired to Pittstown, and finally to Haddonfield, where they presently dissolved.

Washington having reached Trenton, was there reinforced by fifteen hundred Philadelphians. Finding Cornwallis pause at Brunswick, he detached twelve hundred men to Princeton, in the hope of checking the British advance. But the English general pressed on with a superior force, and no alternative was left but to fight or to cross the Delaware. An engagement was not to be thought of; the latter course was accordingly adopted. As the American rear-guard pushed from the Jersey shore, the van of the British came in sight. Washington having taken the precaution to secure all the boats on the Delaware, Cornwallis was unable to pursue the retreating Americans; upon which he determined to close the campaign, and go into winter quarters, occupying various points above and below Trenton. Washington rested on the western bank of the river, keeping a vigilant watch over the fords by which the enemy might be expected to cross.

The American general was in the mean time strenuously endeavouring to augment his force. During his hasty and anxious retreat, he had repeatedly ordered Lee to pass the Hudson and unite with the main army; but apparently anxious to retain his separate command, that ambitious officer had tardily obeyed. Opposing the judgment of Washington, he proposed to take stand at Morristown. Ordered again to march, he moved reluctantly toward the Delaware, by a road some twenty miles west of that pursued by the British. Having indiscreetly quartered at a distance from his troops, information was given by a countryman to Colonel Harcourt, who, with a body of British cavalry, formed and executed the design of making him prisoner. Unaware of the enemy's approach, and protected by but a slight guard, Lee was easily captured. Lee's services had been estimated highly, and the misfortune of his capture cast a deeper shade upon the despondency of the Americans.

The cause of American independence seemed

now to be utterly hopeless. The little army under Washington could with difficulty be held together. But the American general was watchful of every opportunity. In the dispersed situation of the British troops, he quickly perceived an exposure to successful attack, and formed a plan to assail, simultaneously, the posts along the Delaware. About fifteen hundred Hessians were stationed at Trenton. The capture or destruction of these was the chief object of the American commander's daring design. The night of the twenty-fifth of December was fixed upon for the movement. Washington proposed to recross the Delaware about nine miles above Trenton, with two thousand five hundred troops, and march down in two divisions, one by the river, and the other by the Pennington road. General Irvine was to cross at the Trenton ferry and secure the bridge below the town, while General Cadwallader was to pass at Dunk's Ferry, and surprise the enemy's posts at Mount Holly.

The night of the twenty-fifth of December was cold in the extreme. The river was filled with floating ice; and snow, rain, and hail were falling heavily. It was nearly three o'clock before Washington reached the Jersey shore. The two columns took up their respective lines of march, and at about eight o'clock in the morning, drove in the outposts of the surprised and startled enemy. Rallied by their commander, they made a brief but ineffectual resistance. So vigorously did both American divisions press forward, that the Hessians could only look around for the safest road to retreat. The light-horse and a portion of the infantry succeeded in escaping by the Bordentown road. The main body fled along the road to Princeton, but were checked by a regiment of Pennsylvania riflemen. Their six field-pieces had been captured early in the action, and now, surrounded and dispirited by the sudden attack, one thousand Hessians laid down their arms and became prisoners of war.

In securing this brilliant and unexpected triumph, the Americans had lost but two privates killed, two frozen to death, and one officer and three or four privates wounded. Of the enemy, about twenty were left dead upon the field, among these was Colonel Rawle, their commander.

But the plan of Washington was not wholly successful. Generals Irvine and Cadwallader were unable to cross the river in consequence of the quantity of ice. Thus the road to Bordentown was left open, and the post at Mount Holly escaped attack. Nevertheless, the success of Washington was of itself sufficient to cheer the hearts of the Americans. Its material results were considerable, but its moral effect, both upon the British and the colonists, was astonishing. The British were suddenly shown that their task was not so nearly completed as they had imagined, while the Americans were as quickly raised from the gloom of despondency to the light of a glorious hope.

CHAPTER XIV.

Washington takes post at Trenton—Cornwallis advances against him—Perilous situation of the American commander—His daring scheme to escape—Attacks and defeats the enemy at Princeton—Subsequent movements of the contending armies—Washington goes into winter quarters at Morristown—Inspiriting effect of the late victories—Outrages committed by the enemy—New Jersey militia take the field—Skirmishes near Springfield and Hillsborough—Washington's proclamation to the disaffected inhabitants—Exceptions taken to it—Legislature convenes—Difficulties in framing a new militia law—Non-resistance principles respected—Dissatisfaction of Livingston—"Council of Safety" appointed—Its extraordinary powers—Bill to confiscate the estates of Tories—Its favourable conditions—Plundering expeditions of the Tories from New York.

Recrossing the Delaware, Washington sent his prisoners to Philadelphia. Startled by the sudden and unexpected stroke they had received, the British broke up their cantonments along the river, and fell back to Princeton, where a large army was soon concentrated under the command of Cornwallis. Informed of this movement, Washington once more crossed the Delaware to Trenton, with the determination of endeavouring to recover the Jerseys. Here he was joined by General Mifflin, with a considerable reinforcement of Pennsylvania volunteers; but even with this addition his army did not number more than five thousand men, of whom one-half had never before been in the field. What was still more disheartening, in that number were the New England regiments, whose term of service was in a few days to expire. By the persuasions of their officers, however, and the promise of bounty, they were induced to re-engage for a further period of six weeks.

Scarcely was this difficulty surmounted, when Cornwallis, on the second of January, 1777, with a force fully equal to Washington's in point of numbers, and far superior to it in discipline, made a sudden advance toward the American lines. As he approached, Washington withdrew across the Assunpink, a small stream flowing into the Delaware at Trenton. The different passages being vigilantly guarded by his artillery, the British were unable to follow; and after a brisk cannonade, which lasted until dark, the belligerents kindled their fires and encamped.

The American commander was now in a perilous position, from which nothing but a masterly and decisive movement could deliver him. To retreat across the Delaware was scarcely possible, and to maintain his present ground would be to hazard the safety of his little army. He summoned a council of war. After some deliberation a daring scheme was planned to gain the enemy's rear, attack their forces still lingering at Trenton, and then destroy their baggage and stores at Brunswick.

Silently sending his own baggage down the river to Burlington, Washington hastened to put his plan into execution. To deceive the enemy as to his movement, fresh fuel was added to the camp-fires, and small parties were ordered to throw up intrenchments within hearing of their sentinels. These arrangements being completed, about midnight the army moved off by a circuitous route to Princeton. So noiselessly was the manœuvre executed that the enemy received no intimation of it until daybreak; while some of the American militia officers, having withdrawn to the rear to obtain an undisturbed sleep, were, on the following morning, totally ignorant of what had become of their comrades.

At Princeton three British regiments had passed the night. Two of these were already on their march toward Trenton, when in the gray of the morning they encountered the American vanguard, composed of militia under the command of General Mercer. A sharp action ensued. The militia soon gave way, and while gallantly endeavouring to rally them, Mercer received a mortal wound. The check, however, was but momentary. Moving up rapidly with the main body, Washington, exposing himself to the full fire of the enemy, headed a fresh and overwhelming charge. The British were in turn driven back, and the two marching regiments separated. The one in advance managed to regain the road to Trenton, and thus escaped; the other fled hurriedly across the fields to Brunswick. Abandoning the pursuit, Washington pushed on to Princeton, where the third regiment had taken post in the college. At first they made some slight resistance, but the American artillery having been brought up, all further struggle was vain, and they yielded. A few, however, escaped by a precipitate flight to Brunswick.

The loss of the provincials in this spirited action was about one hundred men, including several gallant officers. One hundred of the enemy were slain, a large number wounded, and upward of three hundred made prisoners.

Scarcely was victory achieved when Washington again found his situation one of extreme peril. His troops were exhausted by their night-march and the fatigues of battle. With the frozen sky of winter above them, many were barefooted, others destitute of blankets, and all thinly or imperfectly clad. Wholly unable to fight, retreat was barely possible. Yet Cornwallis was close upon them, with an army in every way superior. Hearing the roar of cannon at Princeton, he had immediately fathomed the intentions of the American chief. Anxiety for the safety of his baggage at once drew his attention to Brunswick. Breaking up his camp at Trenton, he pushed forward so rapidly that Washington but narrowly escaped his vigorous onset. Wisely abandoning his contemplated attack on Brunswick, the latter sought a less exposed situation, where his soldiers would be enabled to find shelter and repose. The hilly country around Morristown offered many strong positions; and, besides, a considerable force of regulars and militia was there concentrated. Accordingly Washington directed his march to that place. Hastily constructing a number of rude huts, he there encamped for the winter, with the main body of the army; Putnam resting with the right wing on Princeton, while Heath, in command of the left, took post in the fastnesses of the highlands. A continuous chain of cantonments kept open the communication between these three points. Meanwhile Cornwallis went into winter quarters at Brunswick.

The triumphs at Trenton and Princeton following one another so closely, and gained by an army that just before had seemed upon the point of breaking up, gave the highest confidence to the American people, not only in the abilities of their commander, but also that their cause would be eventually successful. Nor was this feeling confined to the colonies. On the continent of Europe, Washington's masterly prudence received the highest commendation.

At home the hopes created as to the favourable issue of the war were such as to wonderfully revive the recruiting service, which had been previously attended with but unimportant success. Though the regiments called for were not filled up, still the organization of a new army proceeded with the fairest prospects.

But it was in New Jersey that public feeling had undergone the greatest and most favourable change, which, however, cannot be wholly attributed to the successes of Washington. Many of the people, doubtful or lukewarm as to the ultimate triumph of the patriots, had either remained at home, or accepted British protection. Yet neither their neutrality nor their protection had saved them from the ravages and plunder of the enemy, during their various marches through the state. Churches and other public buildings, as well as private residences, with all their furniture, were destroyed in the most wanton manner. Neither old age nor the weakness of womanhood protected from outrage. Children and infants, and gray-haired men and matrons, were stripped of their clothing, and left to shiver in the cold of winter; while the violation of females, even of a tender age, added the last drop that caused the cup of their bitterness to overflow.

At once the country rose upon the invaders. The wanton outrages of the royal army effected that which the eloquence of Livingston, united with the entreaties of Washington, had all along been incapable of producing. The militia of New Jersey were aroused to shake off this apathy; and from this period until the close of the anxious and weary struggle, no body of men acquired a more favourable reputation, or conducted themselves with a greater degree of disciplined activity and spirit. Eagerly joining the parties sent out by Washington, or acting independently under their own leaders, they performed valuable service in harassing the British outposts, and in breaking up the numerous bands of Tories that infested many portions of the state.

A few days subsequent to the fight at Princeton, Colonel Spencer, with some forty or fifty of the militia, surprised an equal number of Hessians near Springfield, and killed or captured the whole party. For his gallantry on this occasion, Spencer was rewarded with the command of a regular regiment.

About a fortnight afterward, General Dickinson received information that some four hundred of the enemy were foraging in the neighbourhood of Hillsborough. Collecting four hundred of the militia, to which were joined fifty Pennsylvania riflemen, Dickinson hastened to cut the party off. They had just crossed the Millstone River, a stream uniting with the Raritan three miles below Hillsborough, when the Americans came up. The river was waist deep, and running rapidly; but the militia, heedless of the rushing waters, dashed forward with impetuous daring. Without unlimbering their cannon, of which they had three, the enemy fled precipitately. So rapid was their flight, indeed, that the Americans could make but few prisoners. Forty wagons, however, more than a hundred horses, and a numerous drove of cattle and sheep remained in their hands as the fruit of victory. The loss of the enemy could not be definitely ascertained, but they carried off many dead and wounded in their light wagons. That of the militia was trifling.

These brilliant though, perhaps, not very important affairs, served to indicate the existence of a sturdier patriotism than the people of New Jersey had hitherto displayed. But, while gratified with such evidences of public spirit, Washington was pained to be compelled to issue a stern decree against "the infamous practice," common to both militia and regulars, "of plundering the inhabitants under the pretence of their being Tories."

Another proclamation, as humane as it was politic, was, on the 25th of January, addressed to those who had submitted to the British, or accepted their protection, requiring them, as the condition of a full pardon, to repair to the nearest general officer, surrender their protection papers, and swear allegiance to the United States. They were, at the same time, discharged from any obligations they might owe to the king.

Claiming that allegiance was due to the state, and not to the confederacy, one of the New Jersey congressmen objected to this proclamation on the ground that it infringed upon state rights. But Congress approved of it, and the legislature of the state presently passed an act framed in a similar spirit. Its results were speedy and cheering; people flocking in from all parts to submit to the authority of the confederacy, and to engage in behalf of that great cause which had called it into existence.

Shortly after Washington had issued the proclamation alluded to, the assembly of New Jersey was again convened.

The first subject that pressed their attention was the passage of a new law to regulate the militia. Washington, through Governor Livingston, had repeatedly urged that "every man capable of bearing arms, should be obliged to turn out, and not be permitted to buy off his services for a trifling sum," as was the case under the law then in operation. "We want men," said he, "not money." But the Quakers of West Jersey were numerous, and non-resistance was one of their most cherished doctrines. Believing that it would be useless, impolitic, and highly oppressive to attempt to force this class of persons to participate in measures directly at variance with the prime points of their religious creed, the assembly, in framing the new militia law, which they presently enacted, would modify this portion of it in no other way than by increasing the sum that was required to purchase exemption from military duty.

Prudent as the course of the assembly will now be regarded, the patriotic Livingston could not view it in a satisfactory light. But the keenness of his disappointment was afterward mitigated in some degree, by the ready concurrence of both houses in his plan for a "Council of Safety," to consist of the governor and twelve of the representatives, with extraordinary powers, to act during the recess of the legislature. This council was authorized to correspond with Congress and with other states, to perform the duties of justices of peace, to apprehend and imprison disaffected persons, and to call out such portions of the militia as they might deem necessary to execute the laws.

Likewise, on the recommendation of Livingston, another bill was presently passed, authorizing the confiscation of the personal estates of all those who still adhered to the British interest; yet allowing such persons a period of grace, in which, upon renewing their allegiance to the state, they might return and take possession of their property.

Many took advantage of this condition, and were restored to all their former rights and privileges; others, however, assembling in and around New York, endeavoured to make up for the loss of their estates by the fitting out of privateers, and by plundering expeditions into their old neighbourhoods. Nor did they stop with these. Deeply incensed against the more prominent patriots, they seized every opportunity to work them injury; and, aided by secret friends, they were enabled to kidnap several of them, and carry them off to the prisons of New York. Retaliation, of course, followed, with all the fierceness of a civil and partisan contest.

CHAPTER XV.

Opening of the campaign of 1777—American stores at Peekskill destroyed—Skirmish at Boundbrook—Washington takes a strong position at Middlebrook—Howe's feint to draw him from his camp—Its ill success—Howe retreats to Amboy—Washington advances to Quibbletown—Howe returns to attack him—Is again foiled—Retires to Staten Island, and embarks for the southward—Perplexity of Washington in regard to his movements—Loyalists on Staten Island become troublesome—Sullivan's attempt against them—Howe lands at the head of Chesapeake Bay—Battle of Brandywine—Wayne surprised at Paoli—Howe enters Philadelphia—Clinton ravages East Jersey—Battle of Germantown—American successes at the north—Movements on the Delaware—American works at Byllinsport captured—Defences near the mouth of the Schuylkill—Donop assaults Red Bank and is repulsed—Re-election of Livingston—Dickinson's attempt against the Staten Island Tories—Fort Mifflin evacuated and Red Bank abandoned—British in full possession of the Delaware—Skirmish near Gloucester Point—Washington goes into winter quarters at Valley Forge.

WASHINGTON had rested at Morristown nearly three months before the British began to give indications of activity. At length Howe opened the campaign in March, by sending a detachment of five hundred men to Peekskill, on the Hudson, where they succeeded in destroying a quantity of stores which the Americans had collected at that point.

At Boundbrook, in the neighbourhood of

Brunswick, a considerable American force had been posted to guard the upper valley of the Raritan. With the design of capturing this detachment, Cornwallis, on the 13th of April, suddenly issued from his camp at Brunswick, with a large body of troops. The American guard not being sufficiently watchful, narrowly escaped a complete surprise. As it was, they lost twenty men, two pieces of artillery, and a small amount of baggage, before they could gain a safe position.

Washington was soon convinced that Burgoyne, who now commanded the British army in Canada, would attempt to force his way, by Lake Champlain and the Hudson, to New York. It was equally clear to him that Howe would endeavour either to push up the North River or to capture Philadelphia. He therefore determined to make such a disposition of his forces that, by the different divisions being enabled to reciprocally aid each other, any one of these expected movements might be counteracted. While St. Clair, with three thousand men, was left at Ticonderoga, and Putnam, at the head of the eastern levies, in the highlands, the commander-in-chief, with the main body of the army, scarcely eight thousand strong, shifted his camp to Middlebrook, behind a range of commanding hills, about twelve miles from Princeton. His new position was one of great strength. From the heights in front a full view could be obtained of the country between Amboy and Brunswick, and he was thus enabled to observe all the important movements of the enemy in that quarter. A body of continentals and New Jersey militia, under General Sullivan, was stationed at Princeton. Arnold, in command at Philadelphia, was employed with Mifflin in preparing for its defence.

Hoping to draw Washington into a general engagement on ground more advantageous for himself, Lord Howe, on the 13th of June, marched out of Brunswick with a powerful army, apparently intending to force his way to Philadelphia. Calling to his aid most of the troops under Putnam, and ordering Sullivan to retire from Princeton to the more elevated and securer grounds of Rocky Hill, the American general drew up his army in order of battle on the heights fronting his camp, and kept a close watch upon the movements of the enemy. Meanwhile the militia had turned out in force, and with an alacrity they had not hitherto displayed.

Finding his feint insufficient to draw Washington from the impregnable position he occupied, and constantly harassed by small parties of the militia, Howe retreated with some precipitation to Amboy, whence he began to pass his troops over to Staten Island, from which, in accordance with his original design, he made preparations to proceed by sea to Philadelphia.

To cover the light parties that had been detached to annoy the retreat of Howe, Washington moved with the main body of the army to Quibbletown; the van, under Stirling, having descended to the low grounds, yet a few miles nearer to the British. Howe immediately prepared to execute a skilful manœuvre to bring on a general engagement, in which, as the Americans were now situated, he was fully confident of obtaining a triumph.

Recalling the troops on Staten Island, he wheeled suddenly around, and made a rapid movement, in two columns, toward the heights and passes on the American left, which he thus hoped to turn. Happily Washington received early intelligence of the British advance. Penetrating immediately the design of Howe, he fell rapidly back to his cherished position at Middlebrook. During this retrograde movement, Stirling encountered the right column of the enemy under Cornwallis. A spirited skirmish ensued, which resulted in the retreat of the Americans, with the loss of a few men and three field-pieces.

Baffled in his main design, and not choosing to attack Washington's present position, Howe withdrew to Amboy, and thence to Staten Island. Amboy, being thus abandoned, was immediately occupied by a division of the American army. On the 30th of June, leaving five thousand troops to hold New York, the British general embarked with sixteen thousand men for Philadelphia.

Under the impression that Howe intended to push up the Hudson and co-operate with Burgoyne, who was already in the neighbourhood of Ticonderoga, Washington marched leisurely toward the highlands; but the British fleet presently appearing off the capes of the Delaware, he retraced his steps through New Jersey and took post in the vicinity of Philadelphia.

Howe disappeared almost as soon as he was observed, nor was the fleet seen again until a month had nearly elapsed. Perplexed and anxious as to the final destination of the enemy, Washington remained at Philadelphia, industriously preparing for its defence.

Meanwhile the British troops left on Staten Island had rendered themselves highly obnoxious. About one thousand, or a third of their number, consisted of several loyalist or Tory regiments, which were stationed at various points on the coast nearest the Jersey shore. Thus posted, they made frequent incursions against the people of New Jersey, whom they plundered without the least scruple; and, at length, in one of these marauding expeditions they carried off twelve of the most prominent patriots in that section of the state. A counter expedition, to capture the loyalist regiments, was immediately planned by Sullivan, who yet remained in New Jersey with his division.

With picked men from his own command, and a few Jersey militia under Colonel Frelinghuysen, numbering in all about one thousand, Sullivan embarked for Staten Island, during the night of the twenty-first of August, and by dawn of the next day had succeeded in landing unperceived by the enemy. Two loyalist regiments were surprised, and many prisoners made; but the alarm had been given, and a body of British regulars was hastening from another part of the island to intercept Sullivan's retreat. In this they were partially successful. The American general had sent off his prisoners in a captured vessel. Discovering British uniforms on the deck of this vessel, some of Sullivan's boats took the alarm and fled. His re-embarkation was thus retarded so long that the rear-guard was attacked by the enemy, and, after an obstinate conflict, compelled to surrender.

The total loss of the Americans in this affair was one hundred and sixty-two. That of the British in killed and wounded could not be obtained, but the number of prisoners brought off by Sullivan amounted to one hundred and forty-one, including eleven officers.

Sullivan had scarcely regained his camp when he received orders to join the main army. Having landed at the head of Chesapeake Bay, Howe was now marching rapidly toward Philadelphia. Advancing to Wilmington, Washington summoned the militia to his aid; but with all the reinforcements he received, the enemy was still superior, even in numbers.

At length, on the 11th of September, having retired behind the Brandywine, the American general there awaited the British army, sixteen thousand strong. His own effective force was but little more than eleven thousand men, many of whom were militia. In the battle that presently ensued, the Americans unfortunately met with defeat. Nine days afterward Wayne was surprised at Paoli; and on the twenty-sixth of September, Lord Cornwallis, at the head of the British and Hessian grenadiers, entered Philadelphia in triumph.

Meanwhile, retaliating Sullivan's attack on Staten Island, Sir Henry Clinton sallied out of New York with three thousand troops, and overran a considerable portion of the eastern section of New Jersey. Finding that the militia were assembling, and threatened by a detachment of continentals, he at length returned to New York, having caused much annoyance and alarm, and plundered the inhabitants of their most valuable live stock, with a loss of but eight men killed and sixteen wounded.

After the fall of Philadelphia, Washington encamped near the Schuylkill, about fourteen miles from Germantown, where the bulk of the British army was stationed. Here he awaited reinforcements. Dickinson and Livingston were busily engaged in arousing the New Jersey militia. Having by his untiring exertions collected a force of nine hundred men, Dickinson was about to join the main army when he received intelligence of another threatened invasion from New York. Proceeding himself, with three hundred men, toward Elizabethtown, he directed the remainder, under General Forman, to cross the Delaware, and join Washington's camp.

Having received this and other additions to his force, Washington planned an attack on the British at Germantown. An attempt to execute this plan on the morning of the fourth of October, though begun with the brightest prospects of success, terminated in the most disastrous failure, with a loss on the part of the Americans of more than a thousand men.

As if to dispel the gloom occasioned by the defeat of Washington at Germantown, the most cheering intelligence presently arrived from the northern army.

Following up the capture of Ticonderoga, Burgoyne had moved on, gaining triumph after triumph. Stark's success over Baum at Bennington, was the turning point in his career of victory. Its effect in reviving the drooping spirits of the Americans was truly magical. Rallying under the standard of Gates, they closed in from all sides upon the unfortunate Burgoyne. After the two battles of Behmus's Heights—the first resulting doubtfully, but the second in a decided American triumph—the British general endeavoured to effect his retreat to Fort Edward. His communications with that place being cut off, his provisions and supplies intercepted, and his fast-thinning army effectually hemmed in by a superior force, Burgoyne was compelled to surrender his whole army to Gates, on the 17th of October.

Meanwhile, after the battle of Germantown, Washington had retired to his old encampment on the Skippack. Though Philadelphia was lost, the Americans were yet in possession of the river below. They had fortified it with great pains. Howe's fleet was already in the lower Delaware, but safe communication with it from Philadelphia was next to an impossibility. The attention of both commanders was therefore almost wholly bestowed upon the Delaware; that of Howe to remove, and of Washington to maintain intact, the obstructions to its navigation.

The fleet having at length, with great difficulty,

reached Byllingsport, twelve miles below Camden, and captured the unfinished American works at that point, Howe concentrated his forces in the immediate neighbourhood of Philadelphia, preparatory to a vigorous assault on the remaining defences of the Delaware.

On a low island of mud and sand, just below the mouth of the Schuylkill, stood Fort Mifflin, held by Colonel Smith of the Maryland line. Opposite, on the Jersey shore, were the fortifications of Red Bank, consisting of extensive outer works, within which was a boarded intrenchment, eight or nine feet high, protected by an abattis, and well provided with heavy artillery. Two Rhode Island regiments, under Greene, composed the garrison. In the channel between the two forts, large timbers, chained firmly together, and with iron-pointed projecting beams, had been sunk to obstruct the passage of the enemy's ships. There were, besides, in the river several small continental vessels, and a gun-boat battery belonging to Pennsylvania, all of which were under the direction of the brave and gallant Commodore Hazelwood. For the British fleet to reach Philadelphia, it was necessary to remove these obstacles. Hoping that, if they could maintain their ground, Howe would be compelled to evacuate that city, the Americans prepared for a desperate and determined resistance.

On the 21st of October, Count Donop, a distinguished German officer, with twelve hundred picked men, crossed the Delaware at Cooper's Ferry, intending on the following day to attack the post at Red Bank. During the morning of the 22d he marched down the Jersey side and made ready to storm the works. Meanwhile, in accordance with the plan of a combined attack, several British war vessels ascended the river as far as the obstructions would allow, and opened a furious and incessant cannonade upon Hazelwood's flotilla and Fort Mifflin.

Late in the evening Donop drew up his column preparatory to a desperate assault upon the main intrenchment of the Americans, into which, abandoning their outer works, they had withdrawn, in number about five hundred, on the first approach of the British. At length, led by their gallant colonel, the enemy rushed with great intrepidity to the attack. They were met by a deadly discharge of grapeshot and musket-balls. Fighting bravely they continued their assault until, involved in darkness and fatigued by their unavailing efforts, they were obliged to fall back in disorder, with a loss of nearly four hundred in killed and wounded. Early in the engagement Donop had fallen mortally hurt at the head of his column. Favoured by the night, the next officer in command, having collected many of the wounded, made good his retreat to

Philadelphia, where he arrived early in the following morning. During this spirited action, the first as yet in which they had repelled an assault, the Americans lost in all but thirty-six men.

Equal ill success had attended the naval attack upon Fort Mifflin. One of the ships engaged in it was blown up; another, having got aground, was set on fire and abandoned; and the remainder were compelled to drop down the river with serious injury.

Five or six days subsequent to this event, the second legislature of New Jersey convened in primary session. Meeting in joint assembly, on the first of November, they re-elected Livingston as governor without a dissenting voice.

About the same time General Dickinson, having collected nearly two thousand of the militia, determined upon another attempt to cut off the loyalist brigade on Staten Island. But, though he observed the utmost secrecy, the enemy by some means became apprized of his design, and saved themselves by withdrawing into works too strong to be carried by assault. After a skirmish with the flying troops, in which three of his men were killed and ten wounded, Dickinson wisely retired from the island. The loss of the loyalists was trifling, and consisted mainly of the few prisoners brought off by the Americans.

Flattering expectations were created by the gallant defence of Red Bank, that it would be possible to keep possession of the river. In the exultation of the moment, Congress voted a sword to each of the three commanders on that occasion. Meantime strenuous endeavours were made to relieve and reinforce the two forts, against which, after a brief intermission, the British had renewed active operations. Concentrating their efforts against Fort Mifflin, they erected several batteries on a neighbouring island, from which they kept up a furious and unceasing cannonade. Toiling by night to repair the breaches made during the day, the beleaguered garrison fought bravely, but without avail. At length the fort was declared untenable, but not until the vessels of the enemy were so close that the fire of their marines swept the platform. Under these circumstances an evacuation was deemed advisable. Accordingly, about midnight on the 16th of November, the garrison was safely withdrawn.

Hopes were yet entertained of holding the fort at Red Bank, but upon the approach of Cornwallis from Philadelphia with five thousand troops, it, too, was abandoned. Taking possession of the evacuated posts, and removing the remainder of the obstructions, the British fleet and army were at length able to communicate.

Having collected a considerable quantity of

fresh provisions; Cornwallis pitched his camp on Gloucester Point. While he was yet at this place a brilliant little action was performed, in conjunction with an equal number of Morgan's riflemen, by about one hundred and fifty New Jersey militia, under the command of Lafayette. Falling upon a picket-guard of the enemy nearly three hundred strong, they put them to precipitate flight, and drove them completely into the camp, killing between twenty and thirty, and wounding a much greater number. "I found the riflemen," wrote Lafayette to Washington on this occasion, "even above their reputation, and the militia above all expectation I could have formed of them."

The campaign of 1777 was now over. After having narrowly escaped a surprise by the British, Washington, on the 12th of December, went into winter quarters at Valley Forge, a high and strong piece of ground on the left bank of the Schuylkill, some twenty miles above Philadelphia.

CHAPTER XVI.

Distress of the American prisoners in New York—Sufferings of the army—Measures taken by the state for their relief—Articles of confederation brought before the legislature of New Jersey—Alliance between France and the United Colonies—Objections of the legislature to the Articles of Confederation—British foraging party under Mawhood enters Salem county—Conflict at Quinton's Bridge—Gallant exploit of Andrew Bacon—British forces a second time repulsed at Quinton's Bridge—Americans massacred at Hancock's Bridge—Correspondence between Mawhood and Colonel Hand—British return to Philadelphia—Expedition against Bordentown—Narrow escape of Lafayette at Barren Hill—Clinton ordered to evacuate Philadelphia—He retreats across the Jerseys—Washington starts in pursuit—Battle of Monmouth Court House—Lee's conduct during the action censured—He is arrested, tried, suspended, and finally dismissed from the service.

MEANWHILE the legislature of New Jersey remained in session, devising means to meet various demands that were now made upon them. The most pressing of these demands related to the condition of the American army at Valley Forge, and to the wants of that class of suffering citizens whom the enemy had carried off and confined in the prisons of New York.

With regard to the condition of the army, it was deplorable. Frequently, during their encampment, the soldiers were destitute of meat, while vegetables and other articles requisite for their health, were procured with difficulty. Nor were their sufferings less from want of clothing. On the first of February, 1778, nearly four thousand men were reported unfit for duty on that account alone. "A man of sensibility," said Livingston to the legislature, "cannot but feel for these brave men, fighting for their country, at this inclement season, many of them without shoes, stockings, warm clothing, and even blankets to lie upon."

Steps were immediately taken by the assembly to meet these emergencies, so far, at least, as it was possible for a single state to move in the matter. For the relief of the prisoners at New York, Abraham Van Neste was appointed a special commissioner, with authority and means to provide them with such necessaries as they most needed; while, to supply the wants of the suffering army, bills were passed to raise a sum of money by taxation, and by leasing the real estate of such persons as had left the state and joined the enemy.

In order to successfully continue the contest in which they were engaged, Congress had already, on the 15th of November, 1777, adopted certain "Articles of Confederation," creating a more perfect union between the thirteen states, under the style and title of the "United States of America." To render these articles binding, it was necessary that they should be first sanctioned by the several states. Brought before the New Jersey legislature, the question of agreeing to them was yet pending, when Governor Livingston, on the 27th of May, communicated to the two houses intelligence of the most cheering character.

From the beginning of the war, an alliance with France had been sought after, but with ill success, by the American commissioners at Paris. Moved, in part, by the tenacity of purpose exhibited by the revolted colonies, and still more by the probability of Parliament's sanctioning certain conciliatory bills in which the right to tax America was virtually relinquished, Vergennes, the French minister, finally concluded with the commissioners of Congress, two treaties, one of defensive alliance, and the other of friendship and commerce.

It was the intelligence of this alliance that Livingston introduced to the assembly, exhorting them to make "but one more spirited and general effort" to "emancipate themselves into complete and uninterrupted liberty." Inspiriting as it was to them, it was no less so to the country at large, entirely neutralizing whatever effect had been expected from the conciliatory bills, and rendering still more determined the resolution of the Americans to be free and independent.

At length, on the 15th of June, a committee from both houses of the New Jersey legislature, having been previously appointed for that purpose, made a full and able report in regard to the new "Articles of Confederation." Several amendments were proposed to the congressional plan of union, the most important of which were to prohibit a standing army in time of peace; to invest Congress with the sole and exclusive power of regulating the trade with foreign countries; and to authorize that body to dispose of vacant and unpatented lands, for defraying the expenses of the war, and for other such public and general purposes. This report having been adopted, and a copy of it forwarded to Congress, the question was for a time suffered to remain at rest.

Meanwhile, as the spring opened, the enemy began to show signs of life. Pressed for provisions, Clinton, now in command at Philadelphia, found it necessary to send out strong foraging parties into the surrounding country, which suffered extremely from the extent and wantonness of their devastations.

On the 17th of March, a British detachment, some twelve hundred strong, under the command of Colonel Mawhood and Majors Simcoe and Sims, having landed at Byllingsport, made a rapid march to Salem, in the expectation of surprising Colonel Wayne, who, with a few American troops, was posted at that place. Unsuccessful in this, Mawhood, at daybreak of the 18th, despatched Simcoe to cut off a small party of the militia under Colonel Holmes, who were intrenched at Quinton's Bridge, on the southern shore of Alloway's Creek, about three miles from Salem. By a successful stratagem, Simcoe drew the militia from their works across the bridge, and into an ambuscade. A fierce conflict ensued. Surprised and outnumbered, and with a loss of forty men, the Americans retreated to their intrenchments, bravely contesting every foot of the way. As their rear left the bridge, one of the most courageous of the party, Andrew Bacon by name, seized an axe, and heedless of the storm of balls that whistled around him, resolutely cut away the draw, thus rendering immediate pursuit by the enemy impossible. Scarcely was this gallant action performed, when the hero of it received a wound by which he was crippled for life. In the mean time, Colonel Hand, with a reinforcement of militia, had arrived on the ground, and now opening upon the enemy a heavy fire from two pieces of artillery, he compelled them to fall back upon the main body at Salem.

Chagrined on account of Simcoe's ultimate failure, Mawhood determined to pass the bridge at all hazards. Accordingly, early in the following day, he attacked it with his whole force. But cheered by their late success, and so posted that both flanks as well as the front of the attacking column, were exposed to their fire, the Americans obstinately stood their ground, and Mawhood, after a desperate attempt to gain his point, was obliged to retreat in considerable disorder.

Late in the evening of the next day, a party of Tories and regular troops, under the conduct of Simcoe, was despatched to surprise a small body of Americans stationed at Hancock's Bridge, about two miles below Quinton's. The success of this expedition was complete and sanguinary. Wearied out, and unsuspicious of danger, the Americans were sound asleep. A few only woke in time to escape. The remainder, between twenty and thirty in number, some yet asleep, others half aroused, and none offering resistance, were bayoneted in cold blood.

But a few hours after this massacre, Mawhood addressed a note to Hand, now in command at Quinton's Bridge, summoning him to lay down his arms and surrender. In case of refusal, he threatened to arm the Tories, and to "attack all the militia wearing arms, burn their houses, and reduce them, their unfortunate wives, and their children to beggary and distress."

"Your proposal," was the American colonel's spirited reply, "we absolutely reject. We have taken up arms to maintain our rights, and we will not lay them down until success has crowned them, or we have met an honourable death. Your plan of arming the Tories we have no objection to, for it will fill our arsenals with arms. Your threat to burn and destroy, induces me to imagine that I am reading the orders of a barbarous Attila, and not of a gentleman, brave, generous, and polished. If executed, it can only render our people desperate, and increase your foes and the American army."

Not choosing to risk another engagement, Mawhood now turned his whole attention to plundering the neighbouring farmers. Having thus collected an immense store of hay, grain, cattle, horses, and other articles, he soon after embarked in his transports, and returned without molestation to Philadelphia.

Early in May, seven hundred British troops were sent up the Delaware. Landing at White Hill, just below Bordentown, they burned a considerable number of vessels, including two unfinished continental frigates, which had been conveyed to that place for safety. After remaining a few hours in Bordentown, during which time they destroyed no little property, and murdered four unresisting prisoners, the British, having collected their plunder, re-embarked, intending to proceed against Trenton. But meeting with unexpected opposition from the militia, they returned hastily down the river to Philadelphia.

While these events were transpiring, Washington was still encamped at Valley Forge, waiting the arrival of the French fleet, which was already on its way to America. Aware of this, Clinton, fearing that the Delaware might be blockaded, meditated an evacuation of Philadelphia. Rumours of such an intention having reached the American camp, Washington detached Lafayette, with two thousand chosen troops, to gain intelligence, and to annoy the rear of Clinton, should he put his rumoured design into effect. Lafayette having taken a momentary position at Barren Hill, some ten miles in advance of the main army, the British commander, observing his isolated situation, sent a much stronger force to cut him off. But, discovering his peril, the young and gallant Frenchman, by a well-timed and dexterous movement, gained a position which the surprise party would not venture to assail.

At length the intention of Clinton to abandon Philadelphia and retreat through the Jerseys to New York, became evident. Washington's plans were soon laid. While Maxwell, with the New Jersey brigade, having united with the militia under Dickinson, was engaged in breaking down bridges and felling trees across the roads to impede the progress of the enemy, the commander-in-chief himself prepared to lead the main army in pursuit, when they should take up their line of march.

Having sent part of his baggage and stores, together with many loyalist non-combatants, by sea to New York, Clinton left Philadelphia on the 18th of June, and, with ten thousand well-appointed troops, commenced his retreat across the Jerseys. The weather was hot and rainy. Harassed in front by Dickinson and Maxwell, and incumbered with a long line of provision and baggage wagons, the enemy moved slowly, spending six days in reaching Imlaystown, fourteen miles south-east of Trenton.

Meanwhile Washington was not idle. Crossing the Delaware at Corryell's Ferry, now Lambertville, he immediately detached Colonel Morgan, with a select corps of six hundred men, to reinforce Maxwell, and marched himself, with the main body, toward Princeton. Doubtful as to the road Clinton would follow, he halted at Hopewell, five miles from Princeton, for the threefold purpose of resting his troops, securing his choice of a position, and of ascertaining what course the enemy would take.

Washington's earnest desire was to give the enemy battle; and his men, though reduced by sickness and privation, badly equipped, and barely outnumbering the British, were equally eager for the contest. But two councils of war, in which the wishes of the chief were seconded by Lafayette, Greene, Wayne, and Cadwallader only out of fourteen general officers, decided it advisable that nothing more should be attempted than to harass the progress of the enemy. At the head of those opposed to Washington's plan, was Lee, whose exchange had been recently effected, and who held the second rank in the continental service. Taking a wide view of the circumstances, Washington resolved, however, upon his own responsibility, to take such measures as might induce a general engagement.

On the 24th of June, Maxwell was further reinforced; and, during the following day, the main army advanced to Kingston. Here certain intelligence was received of Clinton's design to march by way of Monmouth Court House to Sandy Hook. One thousand additional troops were immediately sent forward to join those already hanging upon the British rear. As Lee, upon whom the command of this division by right devolved, declined accepting it, Washington intrusted it to Lafayette, ordering him to press upon Clinton's left, and crowd him down into the low grounds.

The same evening the main body moved on to Cranberry. A heavy rain-storm and excessive heat delayed its march on the 26th, but that night the advanced corps rested within five miles of the British rear.

Clinton having now brought his best troops to the rear, Washington determined to reinforce still farther his leading column. Accordingly, on the 27th, Lee was sent forward with two brigades. He, of course, took command of the whole advanced division, now swelled to about five thousand men. That evening the commander-in-chief encamped within three miles of Englishtown, where Lee was resting with the advance.

Clinton at the same time took a strong position on the high grounds in the vicinity of Monmouth Court House, or Freehold; his right resting in the borders of a small wood, while a dense and somewhat extensive forest sheltered his left. Another wood protected his entire front. Twelve miles distant were the Heights of Middletown, which he was anxious to gain; for if he could once reach them, he knew that he would be unassailable.

In the gray of Sunday morning, the 28th of June, Washington received information that the enemy were marching off toward Middleton Heights. Anticipating this, he had ordered the advance to be ready to move at a moment's notice. Promising to support him with the whole army, he directed Lee to assault the British rear, "unless there should be powerful reasons to the contrary." Lee at once pushed on to obey; but, confused by contradictory intelligence, it was ten o'clock before he came up with the enemy. Received by a galling fire, his troops, after a series of disastrous manœuvres, fell back, and no steps being taken to check this retrograde movement, the whole division was soon in full retreat.

Washington was, in the mean time, hurrying up with the main army. About noon, after a march of five miles, he met the broken regiments of the advance. His indignation was extreme. Riding to the rear, he encountered Lee. Abruptly, and in a tone of stern reproach, he asked the meaning of the confusion and retreat he beheld. Lee replied with haughtiness; when, uttering a sharp reprimand, Washington rode disdainfully by, rallied the flying troops, placed them in line, ordered Lee to take command, and hurried back to form and bring up the main division.

The aspect of affairs was now changed. Though furiously attacked by the enemy, Lee maintained his ground until the second American line was formed, when he effected an orderly retreat. Washington's second line was next assailed; but, as the British crossed a morass in front, Stirling's artillery, opening from the left, and aided by several infantry corps, effectually checked their advance in that direction. Repulsed at this point, the enemy turned upon Greene, who commanded the right wing; but here again they were met by artillery, the fire from which swept their files, and a second time brought them to a stand. At this juncture Wayne came up with a body of infantry, attacked the assailants in front, and drove them back to the position they had occupied in the morning.

The day was now far advanced. Both armies were utterly exhausted. During the contest the heat had been excessive; so much so, indeed, that numbers of the combatants on both sides had fallen upon the field dead, without a wound. Washington, however, determined to renew the fight at once, and become the assailant in turn. But before his plans could be perfectly arranged, the night came on, and further operations were postponed until the next day. The whole army laid upon their arms on the field of battle, ready to make a new effort for the victory they had so nearly won. But when the morning dawned, Clinton was many miles upon his way to the Highlands of Nevisink. Pursuit was vain. Thus ended what narrowly missed being one of the most momentous battles of the War of Independence.

Upon the field the enemy left four officers and two hundred and forty-five privates dead, and their total loss in killed and wounded could not have been less than four hundred. That of the Americans was three hundred and thirty-two, of which seventy were killed outright. Independently, however, of their loss in the action, the British were materially weakened during their retreat, when full a thousand of their number, principally Hessians, who had married in Philadelphia, took occasion to desert.

Clinton safely reached the Highlands of Middletown, whence, in a few days, he marched to Sandy Hook. From his position at this place, he found a speedy passage to New York in the fleet of Admiral Howe, who had just arrived from Philadelphia with the stores and baggage, narrowly escaping the French squadron, under D'Estaing, which appeared off the Delaware a few days later.

Lee's conduct during the recent action was severely condemned; more so, perhaps, than it justly deserved. Though the indecisive character of the battle was properly to be attributed to his retreat, Washington would probably have overlooked the whole affair; but the pride of Lee had been wounded by the public rebuke of his chief, and the day after the action he wrote Washington a highly disrespectful letter. Washington's reply elicited a second letter, still more arrogant in its tone. Lee was presently arrested and tried by a court-martial, for disobedience of orders, for making an unnecessary, disorderly, and shameful retreat, and for writing two disrespectful letters to the commander-in-chief. He defended himself with remarkable ability; but the court, acquitting him of having made a "shameful" retreat, found a verdict of guilty as to the remaining charges, and sentenced him to be suspended for a year. Scarcely had the term of his suspension expired, when Lee addressed an insolent letter to Congress. For this he presently apologized, but Congress at once dismissed him from the service.

CHAPTER XVII.

D'Estaing arrives with a French fleet—Sullivan's unsuccessful attempt against Newport—Massacre of Baylor's cavalry regiment near Tappan—British expedition against Little Egg Harbour—Chestnut Neck burned—Pulaski's legion surprised in the vicinity of Tuckerton—New legislature elected—Livingston re-chosen governor—Articles of confederation approved—French fleet sails for the West Indies—Campaign of 1779—Difficulty with the Jersey brigade—Capture of Stony Point by the British—Recaptured by Wayne—Major Lee surprises the English garrison at Paulus Hook—Sullivan's expedition against the Indians of New York—Fierce partisan contest in New Jersey—Operations in the south—Financial difficulties of Congress—New Jersey legislature orders nine millions of dollars to be raised—Distress of the American army at Morristown—Washington's requisition upon New Jersey for supplies—Unsuccessful attack upon Staten Island.

Soon after the battle of Monmouth, Washington crossed the Hudson and encamped at White Plains. Learning that D'Estaing had arrived with a fleet and four thousand troops, he concerted with him an attack upon New York. Forced to abandon this enterprise, Washington directed his attention toward Newport, where Pigot, with a large body of the enemy, was now stationed. Having collected New England militia and continentals to the number of ten thousand, Sullivan, to whom the attack upon Newport was confided, only waited for the co-operation of D'Estaing. But as the French admiral, who had put to sea in hopes of meeting the British squadron, was about to engage with Howe, a fierce tempest sprung up, separated the contending fleets, and drove that of France, badly damaged, into Boston. In the mean time, Sullivan had advanced to within a short distance of Newport. Here he received intelligence of D'Estaing's ill-fortune, and was compelled, much to his mortification, to abandon his works and retreat to the main land.

Nearly a month later, in September, two columns of the enemy, conjointly eight thousand strong, left New York and ascended the Hudson by either bank, with the twofold design of collecting forage, and of diverting attention from a proposed expedition against Little Egg Harbour. On the night of the 27th, the advanced corps of the western column, commanded by Major-General Grey, moving with silent celerity, succeeded in surprising a party of American light-horse, under Lieutenant-Colonel Baylor, who were sleeping soundly in a barn near Tappan, in the county of Bergen. So suddenly and unexpectedly did the British appear, that Baylor's men were unable either to fly or to resist. They supplicated for quarter; but were bayoneted almost without mercy. Out of one hundred and four privates thirty-seven only escaped. Of the remainder, twenty-seven were killed and wounded; among the latter of whom was Baylor himself. By the humanity of one of Grey's captains, forty were made prisoners, in disobedience to previous orders to allow no quarter. This massacre, as it was called, stirred up a feeling of fierce indignation against the British, who, however, apologized for it, by pleading the excitement of a surprise and a night attack.

In the mean time, the southern expedition having landed at Little Egg Harbour, on the 5th of October, destroyed thirty prize vessels lying in port, burned the village of Chestnut Neck, and ravaged all the surrounding country. To check this movement, Pulaski's legion had been ordered into the neighbourhood; but it did not arrive until three days after the landing of the British. While encamped in the vicinity of Tuckerton, Pulaski's picket guard was surprised through the treachery of a deserter, and every man composing it—thirty in all—put to death. Gathering up his cavalry, the fiery Pole started in pursuit of the enemy, who had immediately begun a hasty retreat, but was unable to overtake them. So closely did he push them, however, that the only sloop of war in the expedition having got aground, was obliged to be set on fire and abandoned, to prevent it from falling into the hands of the Americans.

On the 27th of October, a new legislature met at Trenton. Having again chosen Livingston governor, both houses, in committee of the whole, proceeded to a renewed consideration of the "Articles of Confederation," to which Congress had once more urged their attention. The subject was earnestly discussed for nearly a fortnight. Declaring that "every separate state interest ought to be postponed for the public good," the committee rose, and, by their advice, the delegates of New Jersey in Congress were immediately instructed to subscribe to the new plan of union. At the same time the committee, in their report, maintained that "the objections lately stated and sent to Congress were founded in justice and equity," and were of the "most essential moment to the interests" of their constituents. For the removal of these objections, they still relied firmly upon the "candour and justice of the several states."

This subject having been thus quietly disposed of, a bill was presently passed to raise the sum of one hundred thousand pounds; after which the legislature took a recess.

The campaign in the north was now, in effect, at an end. D'Estaing, with the French squadron, left Boston for the West Indies on the 3d of November. Upon the same day, five thousand British troops, escorted by a formidable fleet, sailed from New York with a like destination. Toward the close of the month, a second British detachment, three thousand five hundred strong, was sent from New York to act against Georgia. Having formed a junction with the forces of the governor of Florida, they captured Savannah, and in a brief period overran the whole state.

Meanwhile, finding that a successful attack upon New York, even with its greatly reduced garrison, would be utterly impossible, Washington went into winter quarters at Middlebrook, hutting his troops in a line of cantonments, reaching from Danbury in Connecticut, across the Hudson at West Point, to Elizabethtown, New Jersey.

Already with a strong foothold in the southern states, the British, retaining the islands about New York, were henceforth to exhibit their more active and important efforts in the south. Yet the force under Clinton at New York and Newport, was still not less than sixteen thousand men, able at any moment, with the assistance of a powerful fleet, to concentrate at either point. Scarcely equal to the enemy in number, the troops under Washington could not be readily brought to bear, with any prospect of success, either upon Newport or New York. In 1779, consequently, the war, not yet fully opened at the south, in the north consisted chiefly of a series of skirmishes.

Early in the year, however, an expedition was planned against the Six Nations, whose recent attacks upon the border settlements of New York and Pennsylvania called for prompt and severe retaliation. The force to be sent into the Indian country, with orders to burn and devastate their villages and cornfields, consisted of five thousand men, under the general directions of Sullivan.

While this army was being concentrated, preparatory to its final march, alarming symptoms of discontent appeared in Maxwell's New Jersey brigade, which formed a considerable part of the proposed expedition. For more than a year these troops had been vainly memorializing the legislature with regard to their extremely necessitous condition. In April, 1779, Maxwell addressed two highly caustic letters to the assembly on the subject; and, soon afterward, wearied out with delay, the officers of one of the regiments, in a brief but pithy memorial, called upon the legislature for immediate relief. Wearing the appearance of a threat, this memorial placed the legislature in a disagreeable quandary, from which it seemed scarcely possible that they could extricate themselves without sacrificing either their dignity or a number of their best officers. But both were saved by a compromise. Promised that their wants should be immediately supplied, the complainants withdrew their memorial, and the legislature presently voted, and paid at once, the sum of two hundred pounds to each officer, and forty dollars to each private.

Preparations for the Indian expedition now went on. On the 22d of August, the whole army was concentrated where the town of Athens, in Pennsylvania, now stands.

Meanwhile, having ascended the Hudson and captured the American works at Verplank's and Stony Point, Clinton, early in July, despatched a marauding expedition against Connecticut, hoping by this means to entice Washington from his stronghold in the Highlands. New Haven was plundered, and Norwalk, Fairfield, and Green Farms wantonly burned. An attack was about being made upon New London, when the enemy were suddenly recalled by intelligence of Wayne's brilliant and successful assault on Stony Point, during the night of the 16th of July. The British ascending the river in force, Washington found it necessary to again abandon the recovered post, after dismantling its fortifications and removing its artillery and stores.

Wayne's surprise of Stony Point was presently followed by an enterprise equally as bold. While Lee, with his legionary corps, was watching the movements of Clinton on the Hudson, he received intelligence that suggested to him the possibility of carrying off the British garrison at Paulus Hook, on the Jersey shore, immediately opposite New York city. The attempt was one of great danger, and could only be successful by secrecy and celerity. Lee's plans were well laid, however, and he possessed the daring to execute them. On the night of the 18th of August, the assault was made. The enemy were taken by complete surprise. New York being immediately alarmed, Lee could not stop to destroy the works; but he effected a successful, though hazardous retreat, carrying off with him one hundred and fifty of the enemy as prisoners. This feat was highly complimented by Washington, and reflected much honour upon the corps by which it was accomplished.

At length, on the 26th of August, the Indian expedition, under Sullivan, commenced its march up the Chemung branch of the Susquehanna. On the morning of the 29th, at Conewawa, now Elmira, about fifteen hundred Indians and Tories, headed by Brant and Butler, were discovered in a strong position on a rising ground, the approach to which in front was defended by a breastwork half a mile long. A brief but spirited action ensued. Outflanked by Poor's New Hampshire regiment, and vigorously assailed in front by Maxwell and Hand, the enemy abandoned their works and fled precipitately and in extreme confusion.

Laying waste the country in his route, Sullivan crossed over to the Gennessee valley, then the centre of the Indian settlements. Two weeks were spent in desolating this delightful region. Eighteen villages, many thousand bushels of corn, and numerous orchards were utterly destroyed. The blow was a grievous one to the Indians, many of whom never returned to the homes from which they were thus expelled. For a brief period their activity was wholly prostrated; but the recollection of the chastisement they had received was soon obliterated by a keen desire for vengeance, and they began again their attacks upon the frontier settlements.

While these events were transpiring, New Jersey had been the scene of a fearful partisan warfare. Marauding bands of Tories from New York and Staten Island roamed through the eastern counties, plundering, capturing, and murdering the unarmed inhabitants; in some instances not sparing even the women and children. To aggravate the sufferings thus inflicted upon the people, parties of freebooters, sallying out from their hiding-places in the pines, robbed and murdered all that fell into their power, with scarcely any regard to the distinctions of Whig and Tory.

But the Americans did not remain idle. Tories

and pine-robbers were alike objects of their sanguinary vengeance. Against the organized expeditions of the former, the militia were prompt to rally, frequently beating them in fair fight. Many of the prominent freebooters, after having made their names a terror, were hunted out, captured, and hung in chains. Others were shot down like wild beasts, and left unburied where they met their death. So fiend-like were the atrocities they had committed, that none expected and none received mercy.

In the mean time, Prevost, commander of the British troops in Georgia, with about three thousand regulars and Indians, made an attack upon Charleston, in South Carolina. Repulsed by Lincoln, the American general, he returned to Savannah, late in June, enriched with a great quantity of plunder.

On the 1st of September, D'Estaing returning from a successful cruise in the West Indies, appeared before Savannah, which he summoned to surrender. Presently joined by Lincoln, a formal siege was opened, with every prospect of success. But a premature assault, on the 9th of October, having resulted in the repulse of the allied forces, with a loss of nearly nine hundred men, the siege was abandoned, and D'Estaing returned to the West Indies.

The intelligence of these events determined both commanders upon strengthening their respective armies in the south. Leaving New York in charge of General Knyphausen, Clinton, late in December, sailed in person for Savannah; while a considerable number of troops was despatched by Washington in the same direction.

From a late day in October, the legislature of New Jersey had been in session, anxiously deliberating upon the involved condition of the finances of the state, and of Congress. In November, resolutions were received from Congress, recommending the several states to raise their respective quota of money, for the purpose of redeeming the continental currency, which, in spite of every effort to the contrary, had depreciated almost to worthlessness. In compliance with this recommendation, nine millions of dollars—estimated according to the value of the currency of the period—were ordered to be raised in New Jersey, by October of the ensuing year.

For the relief of his army, which was almost reduced to a starving condition, Washington, from his winter quarters at Morristown, presently issued a requisition couched in somewhat harsher terms. Each county in the state was called upon to furnish the camp with a certain quantity of flour and meat. Urging the invincible necessity for these supplies, the commander-in-chief stated that he would be compelled to use force in obtaining them if they were not furnished voluntarily. But, greatly to their honour, the state authorities took the matter in hand. The requisition was speedily answered, and the employment of force rendered unnecessary.

Thus relieved from the pressure of immediate want, Washington again set on foot an expedition against Staten Island, where twelve hundred British troops were quartered for the winter. A passage to the island was now easy, even for artillery, over the ice, which the almost unparalleled severity of the season had formed between it and the main land. Every arrangement had been completed, and Stirling, in command of the expedition, was about to leave the shore, when intelligence was received that the enemy, reinforced from New York, were fully prepared for successful resistance. Consequently, three days afterward, on the 17th of January, 1780, Stirling deemed it advisable to fall back upon the main army, which he did, not unmolested, however, by the British cavalry, from the charges of which he suffered a slight loss in the early part of his retreat.

CHAPTER XVIII.

Campaign of 1780—South Carolina invaded and overrun by the British—Discontent in Washington's army—Knyphausen lands at Elizabethtown Point—Marches toward Springfield—Burns the village of Connecticut Farms—Retires to the Point—Is joined by Clinton—Patriotism of the Rev. James Caldwell—He becomes obnoxious to the Tories—His wife is murdered by a refugee, during the attack on Connecticut Farms—He is shot by a sentinel at Elizabethtown Point—Clinton advances against Springfield—Is met by Greene—Springfield burned—Clinton retires to Staten Island—Arrival of Rochambeau—Gloomy opening of the year 1781—Revolt of the Pennsylvania line—Part of the New Jersey brigade mutinies—Mutineers shot—Cornwallis in the south—Battle of Cowpens—Battle of Guilford Court House—Green partially recovers South Carolina—Cornwallis enters Virginia—Fortifies himself at Yorktown—Is besieged by the allied armies, and the fleet of De Grasse—He capitulates—Prospect of peace—Tory outrages in New Jersey—Murder of Captain Huddy—Peace.

The campaign of 1780 opened in the south. On the 12th of May, Charleston was surrendered to the British forces under Clinton, after the garrison had obstinately sustained a vigorous siege of more than a month's duration. By the middle of June, the whole of South Carolina was in the hands of the enemy. Leaving Cornwallis in charge of the re-established royal government, Clinton returned to New York.

Meanwhile Washington was struggling to put

the northern troops in a condition to co-operate with the French fleet and army, which were expected to arrive early in the summer. In performing this duty, he found many difficulties to overcome. Scantily supplied, and poorly paid in a depreciated currency, the troops were filled with discontent. So alarming, indeed, was the spirit of insubordination they exhibited, that, at one time, it seemed doubtful whether they could be prevented from disbanding.

Highly coloured statements with regard to the tendencies of this discontent were carried into New York, and along with them others, greatly exaggerating some few complaints of the people of New Jersey, occasioned by Washington's late requisition. Hoping to win over the dissatisfied troops and people to the British standard, Knyphausen, on the 6th of June, landed five thousand men at Elizabethtown Point, and advanced through the country toward Springfield. Everywhere, however, he met evidences that he had been deceived. The militia were prompt to take up arms against him; and at Connecticut Farms, four miles from Elizabethtown, he was compelled to order a halt. Incensed by the unexpected opposition they had received, his soldiers fired this beautiful little village, which, together with its church and parsonage, was reduced to ashes. Washington soon after appearing in force, Knyphausen fell back to Elizabethtown Point, where he was presently joined by Clinton, with six thousand additional troops.

During the halt of the British at Connecticut Farms, an outrage was perpetrated that thrilled the entire confederacy with horror and indignation.

Prominent among the American patriots was the Rev. James Caldwell, pastor of the Presbyterian church at Elizabethtown. Of a fiery, energetic nature, and an enthusiastic lover of liberty, he had, at the opening of the War of Independence, ardently espoused the cause of the colonies. Elected chaplain of the Jersey brigade, his zeal and activity won for him the esteem and confidence of the commander-in-chief, by whom he was presently appointed to the commissary department. Faithfully performing his public duties, he did not neglect those of his religious mission. A pure Christian, an ardent patriot, and a practical philanthropist, he soon became a general and well-known favourite with the army and the people.

But the same qualities that gained him the love of the Americans, made him a conspicuous object of hatred to the enemy. To the Tories, especially, he became extremely obnoxious, and they offered large rewards for his capture. When the village of Connecticut Farms was destroyed, his church and parsonage were the first buildings to which the torch was applied. The night previous, Caldwell, hearing of the enemy's approach, had proceeded to Washington's quarters, having first endeavoured in vain to induce his wife, a most excellent and exemplary woman, to accompany him. Trusting that her sex and unprotected condition would save her house from pillage and herself from insult, Mrs. Caldwell, as the enemy entered the village, retired to her room, and there, surrounded by her children, and with an infant in her arms, was engaged in prayer, when a private of one of the loyalist brigades came to the window, and discharged his musket into the group. The unfortunate mother received the ball in her breast, and instantly expired. Her lifeless body being carried into the open street, the house was then fired.

Late in the evening Caldwell observed two soldiers whispering together. His attention was drawn to them by their frequent repetition of "Mrs. Caldwell," which were the only words he could hear. Foreboding evil, he besought them to tell him the worst. It was thus he gained the first tidings of the tragic fate of his wife.

For more than a year subsequent to this mournful event, the patriotic minister continued to perform his religious and military duties with untiring zeal. Late in November, 1781, he was cut off in the vigour of manhood, and in the midst of his usefulness, by a fatality as sad as it was sudden and unexpected. Having gone in his carriage to Elizabethtown Point, to meet a young lady coming on a visit from New York, he was there shot through the heart by a sentinel belonging to the state militia. Morgan, the sentinel by whom he was killed, was immediately arrested and tried. He defended himself upon the ground of having done no more than his duty. But it being proved in court that he had been bribed to the deed by Caldwell's Tory enemies, he was convicted of wilful murder and hung.

Marking his design by a demonstration against West Point, Clinton, on the 23d of June, advanced toward Springfield with six thousand men, intending to make an attempt to carry off the American stores at Morristown. At the bridge over the Rahway, a small stream covering the town, he was met by Greene, with a detachment of fifteen hundred continentals, mostly of the Jersey Brigade, and a few militia. After a gallant struggle, overpowered by numbers, the Americans were compelled to retreat, which they did, though in good order. Retiring to some heights a short distance in the rear, Green took up a strong position, which Clinton, discouraged by the stern resistance he had already encountered, did not venture to assail. Having reduced the thriving village of Springfield to ashes, he fell back to Elizabethtown Point, and thence crossed over to Staten Island. In this battle the American loss was seventy-two in killed and wounded.

Early in July the expected French fleet, having on board six thousand troops under Count de Rochambeau, arrived in the harbour of Newport; but as both army and fleet were immediately blockaded by a superior naval force of the British, Washington's plan of co-operating with them against New York was frustrated.

This third unsuccessful attempt at co-operation with their French allies, the disastrous defeat of Gates in South Carolina, and the treason of Benedict Arnold, following each other in rapid succession, were extremely disheartening to the Americans, and with them the close of the year was a period of the deepest gloom and anxiety.

No brighter, but rather a darker prospect opened with 1781. Under the severest trials the soldiers of the continental army had hitherto exhibited no very wide-spread spirit of insubordination. But toward the close of December, 1780, an angry discussion sprung up in the Pennsylvania line, quartered near Morristown, which finally led to an alarming revolt. With their pay greatly in arrears, and suffering severely from a want of proper food, clothing and shelter, the troops grew discontented; and, alleging that they had enlisted for three years, *or* the war, they demanded to be discharged on the

31st of December, when the three years of their enlistment would expire. The truth, however, seems to have been, as contended by the officers, that the terms under which the greater portion enlisted, were for three years *and* the war. Consequently their demand was refused.

On the 1st of January, 1781, thirteen hundred men paraded under arms, declaring their intention to march to Congress, and obtain redress for their grievances. While endeavouring to restrain the mutineers, one officer was killed, and several wounded. Presenting his pistols as if about to fire, Wayne then ordered them to return to their duty. Their bayonets were immediately at his breast:—"We love you, general," was their declaration, "but if you fire you are a dead man. We are not going to the enemy. Should they approach, we will fight them under your orders. But we are resolved to obtain our just rights." Under the leadership of a board of sergeants, they then marched off to Princeton, where Wayne vainly attempted to bring them to terms.

The crisis was a startling one, and as alarming to the Americans as it was gratifying to their enemies. Informed of the revolt, Clinton despatched his emissaries to the camp of the mutineers, with liberal offers to induce them to enter the British service. But these agents were arrested, handed over to Wayne, and presently shot as spies. Patriotic as was the feeling which in this case guided the insurgents, there were yet doubts that it would long endure.

Entertaining these doubts, Congress wisely bent to the storm. As terms of accommodation, the mutineers were offered, and presently accepted, the discharge of those enlisted for three years or the war; certificates for the depreciation of their pay; the promise of a speedy settlement of all arrearages; and an immediate supply of certain articles of clothing. They then marched to Trenton, where almost the whole line was discharged, without consulting the contracts of enlistment, in regard to which it was deemed expedient not to be too particular. Subsequently, however, these documents were examined, when it was ascertained that, of the men discharged, the greater portion had engaged for the war.

Scarcely was this difficulty surmounted, when, stimulated by the success of the Pennsylvanians, a part of the Jersey line, stationed at Pompton, rose in arms, and advanced similar claims for redress of grievances. A committee, previously appointed by the State legislature, offered to examine into their claims, if the mutineers would submit to their officers. Some returned to their duty, but most remained under arms, demanding to be discharged on their own oaths, as the troops engaged in the late revolt had been.

Mortified at the termination of the previous insurrection, Washington determined to crush at once a spirit so threatening to the integrity of the army. Confiding in the fidelity of the eastern troops, he sent from West Point a detachment, by which the camp of the mutineers was secretly and suddenly surrounded. Their unconditional submission was then demanded. Intimidated by this prompt and energetic movement, they yielded immediately. By their own officers three of the most prominent leaders were pointed out. Arrested and tried by a drum-head court-martial, they were sentenced to death. Mitigating circumstances gained a reprieve for one of the number, but the other two were shot on the field, by a platoon drafted from their own regiment.

Under such discouraging circumstances, Washington prepared for the campaign of 1781. With all his endeavours, the 1st of June found him with but fourteen thousand men in camp. Threatened on all sides by superior numbers, it seemed scarcely possible that he could keep the field for another season.

Meanwhile, from an early period in the year, an active warfare had been carried on in the Carolinas. Having collected a considerable body of troops, Greene, the successor of Gates in command of the southern American army, prepared for a vigorous campaign, by despatching

Morgan, with a thousand men, to harass the British left and rear, lying west of Broad River, in South Carolina. Cornwallis immediately sent Tarleton, his favourite cavalry officer, in pursuit. Retiring before the enemy, Morgan at length took a stand at the Cowpens, where, on the 17th of January, a sanguinary battle was fought, terminating in the defeat of Tarleton, with the loss of more than half his troops. Cornwallis now turned upon Greene, who, having presently effected a junction with the victorious Morgan, for more than a month avoided an engagement; but, at length, on the 15th of March, both armies joined battle in the vicinity of Guilford Court House, North Carolina. Though victorious, Cornwallis, too much weakened to reap the fruits of his success, fell back upon Wilmington. Greene immediately adopted the bold plan of retaking South Carolina. Advancing rapidly toward Camden, he was met and momentarily checked by Lord Rawdon, at Hobkirk's Hill. Adhering to his original intention, however, he finally forced the British from their outposts into the immediate vicinity of Charleston.

Meanwhile Cornwallis, penetrating Greene's design too late to frustrate it, wheeled to the northward, and joined the British troops engaged in ravaging Virginia. After a series of movements against Lafayette, who had been sent to oppose him, he retired across James River to Yorktown, where, in obedience to the orders of Clinton, who apprehended an attack upon New York, he intrenched in a strong position, to await further directions.

Washington had been actively preparing to attack New York, in conjunction with the French army under Rochambeau; but, being informed that a fleet might be daily expected to arrive from France, he at once conceived the plan of a combined naval and military assault upon the position of Cornwallis. Late in August, De Grasse, with the ardently hoped for squadron, sailed into the Chesapeake. In an interview between Washington, De Grasse, and Rochambeau, the plan of operations was speedily arranged. Marching with great rapidity and secrecy, the land forces were already at the head of Elk, before Clinton could believe that any thing more than a feint was intended. By the help of the French transports, the allied armies soon effected a junction with Lafayette, at Williamsburg, whence, in number about sixteen thousand, they marched to invest Cornwallis.

Every arrangement being completed, on the night of October the 6th, the besiegers commenced their first parallel. During eleven days the attack and defence were both conducted with the utmost courage and skill. Cornwallis, however, could maintain his position no longer; while his retreat was effectually cut off by De

Grasse. If the Americans were to storm his works, he could not doubt but that they would be successful. To save the unnecessary effusion of blood that would attend such an assault, he proposed a cessation of hostilities, and terms of capitulation having been finally agreed upon, the garrison, to the number of seven thousand men, surrendered themselves prisoners of war, on the 19th of October.

From the day upon which Cornwallis capitulated, the prospect of a peace, favourable to the independence of the confederated states, grew every moment brighter. The War of the Revolution was virtually terminated. In the south, however, a spirited partisan contest was maintained for a considerable length of time; while, under the direction of the New York Board of Associated Loyalists, numerous bands of Tory refugees continued to harass the people of New Jersey, by a series of wanton and sanguinary outrages. Prominent among these was the murder of Captain Joshua Huddy, a brave and enterprising militia officer from the county of Monmouth—a deed which, though the perpetrators of it were acquitted by a British court-martial, Carleton, the successor of Clinton, reprobated in the strongest terms.

Early in 1782, a resolution was adopted by the English House of Commons, denouncing as enemies to the king all who should advise or attempt a further prosecution of war on the continent of North America. A change of ministry and propositions for negotiation speedily followed, and on the 30th of November a provisional treaty of peace, to take effect when Great Britain and France should conclude an amicable arrangement, was signed by the English and American commissioners at Paris. On the 20th of January, 1783, preliminary treaties between Great Britain, France, and Spain, were agreed to. Peace being thus ensured, Congress, on the 11th of April, proclaimed a cessation of hostilities; and on the 30th of September the independence of the confederacy was formally acknowledged and ratified.

CHAPTER XIX.

Embarrassed situation of the country—Conditional cession of public lands by Virginia—Objected to—Grounds of New Jersey's objection—Virginia withdraws her condition, and the cession is accepted—Federal impost proposed—Favoured by New Jersey and other states—Defeated in consequence of the opposition of New York—Ill feeling thus created—Embarrassing resolution of the New Jersey legislature—National convention recommended—Meets at Philadelphia—"New Jersey Plan"—"Virginia Plan" adopted—Constitution submitted to the states—Ratified by the New Jersey convention—Republican and Federal parties—Politics of New Jersey—Washington chosen president—His journey from Mount Vernon to New York—His reception at Trenton—Trenton established permanently as the capital of the state—Death of Governor Livingston—William Patterson governor—Is made an associate judge in the Supreme Court of the United States—Resigns the executive of New Jersey—Is succeeded by Richard Howell—New partisan differences—Alien and sedition laws—Decline of the Federalists—Joseph Bloomfield elected governor of New Jersey by the Republicans—Removal of the Brotherton Indians.

On the return of peace and the recognition of their independence, the people of the United States had expected to enjoy a period of repose and prosperity. But numerous difficulties of the most disheartening character were yet to be surmounted. Burdensome state and national debts were to be liquidated, conflicting interests reconciled, and mutual jealousies allayed. Dissensions speedily arose; which, for a time, threatened to involve the country in the miseries of anarchy and civil war. Happily, however, eight years of common suffering had so assimilated the diverse population of the several states, that all considerations of a sectional or private nature were at length laid aside for measures conducive to the good of the nation, and to the permanent establishment of its independence.

Even before the ratification of peace, Congress directed its chief endeavours to liquidate the public debt, which formed the most serious obstacle to the prosperity of the country. Already Virginia had ceded to the confederacy a portion of her public lands, to be appropriated to that purpose; but with the condition that her right and title to the remainder should be fully guarantied. To this condition, however, there was no little objection.

In the protracted struggle for independence, the people of New Jersey had exerted themselves to the utmost of their ability. During nearly the whole period of the contest, the main army of the confederacy being within or on the borders of their state, they were at no time free from the unavoidable evils of war. The inhabitants of South Carolina alone had suffered to a similar extent by the depredations of the enemy, while no state had contributed more largely than New Jersey toward supplying the American troops with the necessaries of life. Plundered by their foes, they received but little compensation from their friends; and when paid at all, it was in a currency almost worthless. The depredations of the former they had resisted by taking up arms; to the requisitions of the latter they had, in general, acceded with commendable promptitude and willingness.

In view of these facts, the legislature of New Jersey protested against the acceptance, by Congress, of the offer of Virginia, with its annexed condition. Wrested from England by the joint efforts of the states, the lands in question, they contended, belonged to the states in common. They therefore urged, as "just and incontrovertible," the claim of New Jersey to a "full proportion of *all* vacant territory," the proceeds of the sale of which were to be applied to liquidating her proportion of the national debt. Other legislatures uniting in this protest, Congress rejected the Virginia cession. Presently, however, that state magnanimously withdrew the condition annexed to her offer, and it was then accepted. Her example was speedily followed by the remaining states, claiming vacant or "crown" lands, and Congress was thus confirmed in the possession of a vast extent of territory. Though the chief object of these grants—the payment of the debt of the confederacy—was not accomplished so soon as it was expected, they yet afforded cheering evidences of a scarcely hoped for harmony of feeling between the several states.

As another means of lightening the burden with which the federal government was oppressed, Congress proposed to the legislatures of the different states, that they should confer upon it the right to levy a moderate specific duty on certain imported articles. New Jersey had already urged the necessity of this measure, while hesitating to adopt the Articles of Confederation; and now her legislature willingly granted the desired authority. But the concurrence of all the states was necessary to its confirmation; and, New York steadily refusing her full assent, the measure was finally defeated.

Considerable ill-feeling was excited in consequence. Placed between two powerful commercial states, from which the greater part of her foreign merchandise was necessarily derived, New Jersey had a grievance peculiarly her own —that of paying the duties which those states severally laid upon the importations she consumed. By the proposed federative system of imposts, she had hoped to remove the disadvantages that operated against her, in consequence of the position she occupied. Her disappointment at the failure of that measure was extreme, and expressed in strong language. On the 20th of February, 1786, her legislature, by resolution, refused positively to pay any more specie into the public treasury, until New York consented to the federal impost. This resolution embarrassed the action of Congress considerably, and was deemed of such importance that a committee was appointed for the express purpose of expostulating with the assembly of New Jersey. Visited by this committee in person, the assembly, "being willing to remove as far as possible every embarrassment from the counsels of the Union," at once rescinded the obnoxious resolution, but made no provision for collecting the money which had been called for.

These events, with others of still greater moment, made it evident to the reflecting statesmen of the country, and even to the mass of the people, that some modification, or complete reorganization, of the federal compact was absolutely necessary. Virginia had already moved in this matter. In accordance with a resolution of her assembly, commissioners from five states, including those from New Jersey, met at Annapolis, in Maryland, in September, 1786, "to consider how far a uniform system in the commercial relations of the United States might be necessary to their common interest, and their present harmony." But, finding themselves few in number, and without adequate authority to adopt any definite and effectual measures, they recommended a convention of delegates from the several states, to meet at Philadelphia, in the following May, and then adjourned.

Congress acquiescing in this call for a convention, the states, moved, probably, by an alarming insurrection in Massachusetts, speedily agreed to it. Virginia first, and then New Jersey, appointed delegates; the latter naming William Livingston, David Brearley, William Patterson, Jonathan Dayton, Abraham Clark, and William C. Houston.

At the time and place appointed, delegates from twelve states assembled. Washington was unanimously chosen president of the convention, which, with closed doors, immediately entered upon the important business before it. During the long and stormy period of its session, three distinct plans were brought up for discussion. The first of these, introduced by Patterson, of New Jersey, and known as the "Jersey" or "State-Rights Plan," proposed, simply, that the Articles of Confederation should be so amended as to confer increased authority upon Congress, without disturbing the original equality of the several states in that body. As a majority of the convention favoured an entire remodelling of the federative system, this scheme was rejected, as was also that introduced and advocated by the celebrated Alexander Hamilton, who proposed the establishment of a purely national government. The "Virginia Plan," a species of compromise between the two rejected schemes, and of a mixed federal and national character, was then taken up, and made the basis of our present constitution, as finally adopted on the 17th of September, 1787.

Submitted to Congress, the new constitution was presently transmitted by that body to the several legislatures, with a recommendation that state conventions, of delegates chosen by the people, should be called to decide upon its approval or rejection.

The New Jersey convention met at Trenton, on the 11th of December. With grave deliberation, the new instrument of union was read over section by section. Scarcely any discussion took place, and no amendments were offered. On the 18th, the constitution was ratified by the unanimous voice of the convention; and, on the following day, the members proceeded in solemn procession to the court-house, where the result of their deliberations was made known to the assembled people. New Jersey was thus the third state to accept of the constitution, having been preceded but a few days by Delaware and Pennsylvania.

The sanction of six more states was necessary, however, to render the new instrument binding upon the confederacy. From the first, the delegates of New Jersey had been decided friends to the doctrine of states-rights; but only, perhaps, so far as the one question of equal representation was concerned. On most other points they appear to have been favourable to a strong national government. Franklin's amendment to the "Virginia Plan," by which, in the higher branch of the confederative legislature, the representation of the several states was rendered equal, had removed their principal objection to the constitution as finally adopted. But, by a considerable proportion of the people of the country at large, amounting, indeed, almost to a majority, a somewhat broader ground of objection had been taken. Many contended that Congress and the president had been invested with powers altogether too extensive; and that these powers had been taken from the individual states. Others went still further, declaring that the new constitution would lead to a breaking up of the Union, and that the convention which framed it had transcended their authority, which was to amend, merely, the old Articles of Confederation. But, at length, New Hampshire having accepted of the constitution, the required number of states was completed, and it thus became the fundamental law of the republic.

As has just been intimated, the whole people of the United States, on the question of adopting or rejecting the federal constitution were at once organized into two widely differing parties. On the one side were the Federalists, who not only declared themselves in favour of accepting the new compact, but also, in some instances, contended that it ought to have been rendered still more centralizing. Between these and their opponents, who presently took the name of Republicans, a warm political warfare was kept up, even after the ratification of the constitution by all the states.

To New Jersey the constitution ensured peace, prosperity, and freedom from the apprehensions of becoming the prey of her more powerful neighbours. Consequently the mass of her people sided with the Federalists, though they do not appear to have been carried into that current of partisan animosity by which their brethren in other parts of the Union were so violently agitated. In Virginia and New York, however, the republicans held an undoubted majority. By these states it was proposed to call a second national convention. But, the Congress of 1789 having adopted certain amendments to the constitution, this proposition was not agreed to by any other state. In the mean time, moreover, Washington, who, though no partisan, was an avowed friend of the new Federal compact, had been elected to the office of President of the United States, and for a brief period there was a lull in the political tempest.

From Mount Vernon to New York, where his

inauguration was to take place, Washington had desired to proceed without display or ceremony. But the whole course of his journey was marked by splendid receptions and entertainments, warm congratulations, and whatever could exhibit the deep veneration and sincere gratitude of the people with whom he came in contact. Though not so magnificent as at other places, nothing could have been more touchingly appropriate than his reception at Trenton, where, twelve years before, he had appeared under circumstances so widely different. On the same bridge over the Assunpink, which he had crossed the night previous to the battle of Princeton, was erected a triumphal arch, supported by thirteen columns, twined with evergreens and flowers, and bearing the inscription—"The Defender of the Mothers will be the Protector of the Daughters." Underneath this arch, Washington, as he entered the town, was met by a procession of matrons, intermixed with whom were young girls—their daughters—clad in white, and each carrying a basket of flowers. When the president drew near, they began to sing the following little Ode, which had been written for the occasion, by Richard Howell, Esq.:—

"Welcome, mighty chief, once more,
Welcome to this grateful shore;
Now no mercenary foe
Aims again the fatal blow,
Aims at thee the fatal blow.

> Virgins fair and matrons grave,
> Those thy conquering arm did save,
> Build for thee triumphal bowers;
> Strew, ye fair, his way with flowers!
> Strew your hero's way with flowers!"

As they sung the last line of their song, suiting the action to the words, they strewed before him a profusion of flowers from their baskets.

Little of marked historical importance occurred in New Jersey for a number of years after the election of Washington to the presidency. During the session of the legislature, in 1790, the seat of government of the state was permanently established at Trenton. In July of the same year, the old and tried governor of the commonwealth, William Livingston, died while yet in office, deeply lamented by all parties. Chosen when the government was first organized, he had remained at his post, without shrinking, during the entire period of the perilous struggle for independence. Having assisted in framing the federal constitution, he became its zealous supporter, and his influence had been exerted with great effect to procure its ratification by the state. He died on the twenty-fifth of July, and was succeeded as governor by William Patterson, who continued in office until March, 1793; when, having been appointed an associate judge in the supreme court of the United States, he resigned. Governor Patterson was succeeded by Richard Howell, who remained in service until October, 1801.

During the period of Governor Howell's administration, a great change took place in the condition of the two political organizations of the state and nation. The original point in dispute had been dropped, and new questions, both of foreign and domestic policy, were brought up, inflaming to the highest degree the animosity of partisans.

Emerging from a bloody revolution, France had proclaimed herself a republic, and, soon after, declared war against England. By the new and ill regulated government, the United States, during a period extending from 1793 to 1798, were subjected to many mortifying insults and grievous injuries. Siding with the French, the Republicans or Democrats, as they now began to be called, advocated the interference of the American government in favour of France, either by taking up arms in her behalf, or by fulfilling the conditions of a treaty made with the late empire, which provided that French privateers and their prizes, but not those of any country at war with France, should receive shelter in the ports of the United States. Deeming this treaty no longer binding, and wishing to preserve the country from the miseries of a foreign war, Washington, supported by the Federalists, issued a proclamation of strict neutrality. Shortly subsequent, several French privateers, fitting out in American ports, were seized by the Federal authorities. Against these seizures, Genet, the minister of the Directory of France, entered a warm protest, and, encouraged by the sympathies of a large portion of our citizens, violently assailed the prudent course of the administration. But, with the recall of Genet, the excitement thus created partially subsided.

France, however, still maintained her insulting and injurious policy. At length, during the administration of the elder Adams, who energetically, but with little avail, endeavoured to obtain redress, the prospect of a war with that country became well-nigh certain. It was on this occasion that the celebrated Alien and Sedition laws were passed, for the avowed purpose of sustaining the policy of the administration. The arbitrary nature of these laws at once brought upon them the obloquy of a considerable majority of the American people, and the Federal party, with which they originated, immediately began to decline. In 1800—but two years after their passage—Thomas Jefferson, the Democratic candidate, was elected to the presidency over Mr. Adams.

Hitherto New Jersey had been strongly Federal, so strongly indeed, that the majority of that party in the legislature, adopted, previous to the election in January, 1801, a general-ticket system of choosing representatives to Congress. They were confident of securing by this means a delegation wholly federal. But the event was contrary to expectation; the Democratic party triumphing with from five hundred to a thousand majority. The state election, in the following October, also resulted favourably to the Democrats. Having obtained a majority in both branches of the legislature, they were enabled to elect their candidate for governor—the humane and popular Joseph Bloomfield.

During the year 1802, the last feeble remnant of the New Jersey Indians, between seventy and eighty in number, removed from the state. While quietly settled at Brotherton, as their little tract in Burlington county was called, a message came from the Stockbridge Indians, dwelling upon the shores of Oneida Lake, in New York, inviting them "to come and eat of their dish, which was large enough for both." "We have stretched our necks," continued the characteristically worded message of the simple red men, "in looking toward the fire-side of our grandfathers, until they are as long as cranes." Accepting this invitation, the Brotherton Indians, having obtained permission to sell their lands, took a final departure from the hunting-grounds of their ancestors.

There being no choice for governor at the

election in October, John Lambert, vice-president of the upper legislative house, performed the duties of that office during the ensuing gubernatorial year. In 1803, however, Bloomfield was again chosen.

CHAPTER XX.

Re-election of Bloomfield—Act for the gradual abolition of slavery—Aaron Burr—Sketch of his life—Origin of his quarrel with Hamilton—He kills Hamilton in a duel—Is indicted for murder by a New Jersey grand jury—His journeys to the West—His arrest, trial, and acquittal—His subsequent career and death—Is buried in the Princeton grave-yard—Difficulties between the United States, England, and France—British orders in council—Napoleon's retaliatory decrees—American Embargo Act—Continued aggressions of England—Affair of the Chesapeake—Hostilities declared—Exemption of New Jersey from invasion—Naval victories of Bainbridge and Lawrence—Death of the latter—American successes—Peace—Governors Aaron Ogden, William S. Pennington, Mahlon Dickerson—School fund created—Isaac H. Williamson governor—Act to expedite the extinction of slavery—Common schools established—Peter D. Vroom governor—Jacksonian and Whig parties—Governors Samuel S. Southard, Elias P. Seeley, Philemon Dickerson—Financial embarrassments—Triumph of the Whigs—William Pennington governor—Constitutional convention—New constitution ratified by the people—Governors Dan. Haines, Charles C. Stratton, George F. Fort—Present condition and prospects of the state—Conclusion.

FROM the period of Bloomfield's second election until the War of 1812, the history of New Jersey affords but few points of interest, as connected with the public action of the state. The political aspect of affairs was decidedly favourable to the Democrats, Bloomfield being re-chosen every year until the opening of hostilities.

Much to the gratification of the governor, who had been from the first an ardent advocate of the abolition of slavery in his own state, on the 15th of February, 1804, an act was passed, with scarcely a dissenting vote, declaring that all persons, the children of slave parents, born after the fourth of July, in that year, should become free—the males, when twenty-five years old, and the females on arriving at the age of twenty-one. Thus New Jersey, the seventh, and, notwithstanding the character of her population, the last of the original thirteen to do so, became virtually one of the circle of free states.

It was during this year that the fatal duel between Aaron Burr and Alexander Hamilton, took place at Weehawken, on the Jersey shore, opposite New York city.

Burr was a native of Newark, and a graduate of Princeton College, of which his father was the first president. Leaving college with the highest academic honours, at the early age of sixteen, he entered upon the study of the law; but the War of Independence breaking out, he joined the American army, in which he rose to the rank of colonel. Having served through two active campaigns, during one of which he took part in the Battle of Monmouth, he grew dissatisfied, threw up his commission, and returned to his legal studies. Daringly ambitious, he had recourse to politics as the speediest and most certain avenue to distinction. His undoubted talents and genius for intrigue, united with polished manners and a singularly fascinating address, brought him rapidly into notice, and he soon became one of the most prominent and popular democratic leaders. In 1801 he was elected Vice-President of the United States.

From the elevation he had attained, Burr fell suddenly. Charged with intriguing against Jefferson, in order to secure his own election to the office of president, he was abandoned by most of his party, which would nominate him neither for re-election to the vice-presidency, nor as a candidate for the executive chair of New York. For the latter station, however, he determined to run independently, expecting to obtain the votes of the Federalists, whose shattered condition rendered hopeless the election of a candidate of their own. But Hamilton, the great leader of the Federal party, though not active against Burr, refused to give him his support, and he was defeated.

Chagrined and disappointed, Burr at once turned upon Hamilton, to whom he attributed his defeat, with the malignant and studied determination of forcing him into a duel. After endeavouring, in every honourable way, to avoid what both his reason and his conscience abhorred, Hamilton at length accepted a challenge from Burr. Early on the morning of the 11th of July, the parties met. At the first fire, Hamilton fell mortally wounded, unconsciously discharging his pistol as he sunk to the ground. For twenty-four hours he lingered in extreme agony, and then calmly expired.

A perfect storm of indignation broke over the surviving principal in this lamentable affair. Public opinion regarded him as but little better than a cold-blooded murderer; and, as such, he was presently indicted by a New Jersey grand jury. Efforts were made to stay prosecution on this indictment, but though he had been a personal friend of Burr, Governor Bloomfield steadily refused to interfere for that purpose. No other course was left to Burr, therefore, than to avoid entering the state.

Ruined in reputation, and with his ambitious hopes forever blasted, the wretched Burr, having served out his unexpired term as vice-president, presently crossed the Alleghanies, and sailed down the Ohio and Mississippi to New Orleans, stopping, very mysteriously, at various points on his route. Returning to Philadelphia in the winter of 1805, he remained there until the following summer, when he again set out for the West. It having at length become evident that his designs were of a treasonable character, his arrest was determined upon, and a reward offered for his apprehension. On the 19th of February, 1807, he was captured, while travelling with a single companion, through the Tombigbee country, in Eastern Mississippi. He was presently tried on the charge of treason against the United States. His guilt could scarcely be doubted, but the evidence against him was informal, and he was acquitted. Indictments for treason were also hanging over several of his associates, among whom was Jonathan Dayton, of New Jersey. These, of course, were now abandoned.

After standing his trial on certain other charges, of which he was likewise acquitted, Burr embarked for Europe, where, for four years, he lived an object of suspicion, and a wretched, restless wanderer. Returning in 1812 to New York, he there resumed the practice of law. His death, at the age of eighty-four, took place on the 14th of September, 1836. His remains were carried to Princeton, and there buried, with the honours of war, beside the grave where repose those of his father.

While Burr was yet engaged in his treasonable plot, the foreign relations of the Union had assumed a troubled aspect.

During the bloody war which succeeded the French Revolution, and up to the year 1806, the United States had enjoyed a prosperous, though not entirely uninterrupted trade with Europe. Various assumptions of exclusive naval authority were, however, from time to time set up by the British government. Among these were the right of search, and the right of impressment, which, at this period, England, attempted to enforce, greatly to the injury of our seamen, native-born as well as adopted citizens. At the same time, that government issued a formal Order in Council, the effect of which was to destroy completely the commercial relations existing between France and America. Incensed by these invasions of the individual rights of their citizens, and of their own commercial rights as a neutral confederacy, the United States energetically remonstrated, through their commissioners, Messrs. Monroe and Pinckney. England, however, continued to insist upon her assumed right to impress American mariners on the high seas, and to force American vessels, engaged in commerce with other nations, to sail under the license of a British admiral, or be subject to capture and confiscation.

Meanwhile, in imitation of his more powerful maritime rival, Napoleon, now Emperor of the French, issued his retaliatory Berlin and Milan decrees; which rendered all neutral vessels trading in English merchandise, or under British licenses, liable to seizure and confiscation by the cruisers of France; just as the British Orders in Council had previously subjected American vessels found trading with French property on board, to capture and confiscation by the navy of England.

Under these irritating circumstances, it was at first thought prudent to withdraw our commercial marine from the ocean altogether. In accordance, therefore, with the recommendation of President Jefferson, Congress, in 1807, passed an act enforcing an embargo on American vessels. This measure was followed by others of a similar character, including the act of non-intercourse; but, contrary to anticipation, they wrought no favourable change in the conduct, either of France or England. On the contrary, the latter nation, especially, seemed to grow more determined in her insolence and in her acts of aggression. Among these last was the wanton attack made by one of her cruisers, the Leopard, upon the American frigate Chesapeake, under the pretence of recovering certain men, claimed as deserters from the British service.

From this period, until 1812, various efforts were made to settle, by amicable negotiations, the irritating questions in dispute between the two countries. But all these efforts having failed, Congress, finding that hostilities could no longer be honourably avoided, formally declared war against Great Britain, on the 18th of June, 1812.

Confined mostly to the frontiers and the ocean, the contest that followed this declaration caused no injury to New Jersey from actual invasion. In other respects she sustained her share of the sufferings and expenses, consequent upon hostilities. In the maritime successes, by which, alone, during the early part of the war, the arms of America were preserved from disgrace, two of her sons gloriously participated; winning names that will not soon be blotted from the list of our country's naval heroes. Of these, one was William Bainbridge, a native of Princeton, and commander of the Constitution, when she made a prize of the British frigate Java, on the 29th of December, 1812. The other was the heroic Lawrence, of Burlington, the captor of the Peacock brig-of-war. But Lawrence's career, which had opened so brilliantly, was suddenly brought to a close on the 1st of June, 1813; he being on that day mortally wounded, during an engagement in which his vessel, the Chesapeake, after a brief but most sanguinary struggle, was compelled to yield to the British frigate Shannon.

It was not until the opening of 1814, that the military arm of our national defence began to recover permanently from its early disasters. During that year, however, it achieved a series of important triumphs in the north-west, on the

Canadian frontier, and in the south. On the 8th of February, 1815, hostilities were finally terminated by the celebrated victory of General Jackson, over the enemy, at New Orleans. Two weeks previous, a treaty of peace had been signed at Ghent; and on the 17th of the following month, it was ratified by the President and Senate.

Meanwhile several slight political changes had occurred in New Jersey. At the state elections in 1812, the Federal or Peace party carried the legislature, secured a majority of the congressional delegation, and elected Aaron Ogden governor. In the following year, however, the Democrats recovered their lost ascendancy, and William S. Pennington was chosen to fill the executive chair.

Pennington was succeeded, in 1815, by Mahlon Dickerson, who remained in office two years. It was during his administration that the first step was taken toward creating a permanent fund for the establishment and support of a system of common schools.

In 1817, Isaac H. Williamson was elected governor, to which office he was annually chosen until 1829. While Williamson occupied the chair of state, two important public measures were adopted. The first of these was an act, passed in 1820, embracing and extending the principles of the abolition bill of 1804. By its operation the extinction of slavery has been greatly hastened. Indeed, at the present time, there are no slaves in the state, though about two hundred persons, the children of slave parents, are still held to labour as "apprentices," under the provisions of the act of 1820.

The second measure above alluded to, was adopted in February, 1829. By it the first common schools in the state were established. For their support, provision was made for an annual appropriation of twenty thousand dollars, to be taken from the income of the fund created in 1816. By the liberality of the legislature, that fund had already been increased to a respectable sum.

In 1829, Peter D. Vroom, Esq., was chosen to succeed Governor Williamson. He was a member of the new Democratic or Jackson party, which had sprung up since the dissolution of the two old partisan organizations in 1827.

For a period of nearly fourteen years after the first election of Vroom, the history of New Jersey affords but few points of interest to the general reader. In 1832, the National Republican or Whig party, organized in opposition to the Jacksonian Democrats, succeeded in carrying the state. Samuel L. Southard, formerly Secretary of the Navy under Presidents Monroe and Adams, was elected to the office of governor; but, he being presently chosen to the United

States Senate, Elias P. Seely, likewise a Whig, was selected to fill the vacancy thus occasioned. In the following year, however, the Democrats again triumphed; Governor Vroom being once more chosen to occupy the executive chair. He remained in office until 1836, when he was succeeded by Philemon Dickinson, a member of the Democratic party.

During this year events occurred which, for a time, materially changed the condition of parties. Financial difficulties of the most distressing character arose, causing the bankruptcy of a large number of mercantile houses, and the complete prostration of almost every branch of employment. By the Whigs it was alleged that these difficulties sprung from President Jackson's opposition to the rechartering of the Bank of the United States; from his removal of the treasury deposits; and from his circular of 1836, ordering all moneys due the government to be paid in specie. Whether these allegations were true or not, as the distress in the country had grown up under a democratic administration, it led to a reaction highly favourable to the Whigs. During the state canvass of 1837, the latter party elected William Pennington as governor, to which office he was annually re-chosen until 1843.

Meanwhile, in the nation at large, the Whigs continued to augment their strength until, in

1840, they elected General Harrison to the presidency with an overwhelming majority. Harrison's death, one month after his inauguration, by placing Vice-President Tyler in the executive chair, caused a vacancy in the speakership of the National Senate, to which the distinguished Southard, of New Jersey, was presently elevated. He thus became, by virtue of his office, Vice-president of the United States.

Though formed hastily during a troubled and stormy period, the constitution of the state had hitherto afforded general satisfaction. During the year 1843, however, there were decided manifestations that some modification of it was desired by the people. Adopted at a time when the colonies had not fully resolved upon independence, it still retained a provision for renewing the colonial connection with Great Britain. This provision was now, of course, a matter of slight importance, yet it appeared singular and out of place, and was offensive to many. But the principal objection to the old plan of government was based upon the fact that it contained, in far too small a degree, those popular elements which, in the constitutions of most of the other states, had been more freely and fully developed.

After some hesitation on the part of the legislature, in February, 1844, a convention of delegates, chosen by the people, was summoned to meet, on the 14th of May then following, in order "to frame a constitution of the state, to be submitted to the people thereof, for ratification or rejection."

On the day appointed for the convention, fifty-eight delegates assembled. After some discussion, it was determined to frame a constitution entirely new. Entering upon its work in a liberal and intelligent spirit, the convention presently submitted to the people an instrument which, while it remained free from the extremes of an excessive zeal for reform, exhibited the full acquaintance of its framers with the advanced political science of the age. Ample security was given for the rights of the people; the different departments of government were made independent of each other; the governor, hitherto chosen by the legislature annually, was now rendered elective by the people every three years; the judiciary was established on a new and more permanent footing; the property qualifications formerly required of the members of the legislature, was entirely removed, and the right of suffrage, restricted by the old constitution to freeholders, was now extended to all free white males above the age of twenty-one years.

Such, in its more important features of improvement, was the new plan of government, as ratified by the almost unanimous voice of the people, on the second Tuesday in August, 1844. From the period of its adoption, until the present time, the history of the state presents few points for the consideration of the historian.

The last governor under the old constitution was Daniel Haines, a member of the Democratic party, and elected in 1843. He was succeeded in 1844 by Charles C. Stratton, a prominent Whig. At the subsequent canvass in 1847, the Democrats were again triumphant, re-electing ex-governor Haines. Since that period the state has remained in the hands of the Democratic party: Governor Fort, the present executive, being a member of that organization.

Having thus brought the history of New Jersey to a close, little remains to be said beyond a brief notice of the present condition and prospects of the state. By the census of 1840, the number of her inhabitants was three hundred and seventy-three thousand, eight hundred and twenty-three. The census of 1850 exhibits a population of four hundred and eighty-nine thousand, five hundred and fifty-five; the ratio of increase during the decade having been thirty-one per cent. Being more than double the average of that of all previous decades since the Revolution, this ratio of increase affords cheering evidence that, as far as regards population, a new and fresh impetus has been given to the advancement of the state.

But it is not in this particular alone that New Jersey exhibits tokens of a vigorous existence. Debarred from foreign commerce, her people have turned their attention to agriculture and manufactures, for which, by the diversity of her soil, and by the number of her mines and water-courses, the state possesses many and rare advantages. In both pursuits her citizens have prospered abundantly, and every year is adding to the wealth and importance which they derive from them.

Since the establishment of the common-school system, the cause of education has been progressing with a rapidity greater even than could have been expected. Though established but little more than twenty years, there are already in the state no less than one thousand five hundred public schools, with an average attendance of eighty thousand children. In addition to these, three first-class colleges, and two theological seminaries, which are attended by between six and seven hundred pupils. Still further, we find two hundred and thirty private academies, attended by more than ten thousand scholars. The number of libraries, public and private, in the state amounts to four hundred and fifty-nine, containing two hundred and sixty-one thousand volumes.

No state in the American Union presents to the consideration of the historian a purer political character than New Jersey. Her soil was obtained from the original proprietors without fraud or oppression in any instance; while in arranging the future government of the province, the wisdom of her early rulers led them to adopt such simple and inexpensive regulations as were best calculated to meet the wants of the people, and to establish firmly among them the principles of peace, justice, and equity.

THE END.

STEREOTYPED BY L. JOHNSON & CO.
PHILADELPHIA.

CATALOGUE
OF
VALUABLE BOOKS,
PUBLISHED BY
J. B. LIPPINCOTT & CO.,
(LATE LIPPINCOTT, GRAMBO & CO.)

No. 20 NORTH FOURTH STREET, PHILADELPHIA;

CONSISTING OF A LARGE ASSORTMENT OF

BIBLES, PRAYER-BOOKS, COMMENTARIES, STANDARD POETS,

MEDICAL, THEOLOGICAL, AND MISCELLANEOUS WORKS, ETC.

PARTICULARLY SUITABLE FOR

PUBLIC AND PRIVATE LIBRARIES;

For Sale by Booksellers and Country Merchants generally throughout the United States.

THE BEST AND MOST COMPLETE FAMILY COMMENTARY.

The Comprehensive Commentary on the Holy Bible;

CONTAINING

THE TEXT ACCORDING TO THE AUTHORIZED VERSION,

SCOTT'S MARGINAL REFERENCES; MATTHEW HENRY'S COMMENTARY, CONDENSED, BUT CONTAINING EVERY USEFUL THOUGHT; THE PRACTICAL OBSERVATIONS OF

REV. THOMAS SCOTT, D.D.;

WITH EXTENSIVE

EXPLANATORY, CRITICAL, AND PHILOLOGICAL NOTES,

Selected from Scott, Doddridge, Gill, Adam Clarke, Patrick, Poole, Lowth, Burder, Harmer, Calmet, Rosenmueller, Bloomfield, Stuart, Bush, Dwight, and many other writers on the Scriptures.

The whole designed to be a digest and combination of the advantages of the best Bible Commentaries, and embracing nearly all that is valuable in

HENRY, SCOTT, AND DODDRIGE.

EDITED BY REV. WILLIAM JENKS, D.D.,

PASTOR OF GREEN STREET CHURCH, BOSTON.

Embellished with five portraits, and other elegant engravings, from steel plates; with several maps and many wood-cuts, illustrative of Scripture Manners, Customs, Antiquities, &c. In 6 vols. super-royal 8vo.

Including Supplement, bound in cloth, sheep, calf, &c., varying in

Price from $10 to $15.

The whole forming the most valuable as well as the cheapest Commentary in the world.

The Companion to the Bible.

In one super-royal volume.

DESIGNED TO ACCOMPANY

THE FAMILY BIBLE;

OR,

HENRY'S, SCOTT'S, CLARKE'S, GILL'S, OR OTHER COMMENTARIES.

ILLUSTRATIONS OF THE HOLY SCRIPTURES,

In one super-royal volume.

DERIVED PRINCIPALLY FROM THE MANNERS, CUSTOMS, ANTIQUITIES, TRADITIONS, AND FORMS OF SPEECH, RITES, CLIMATE, WORKS OF ART, AND LITERATURE OF THE EASTERN NATIONS:

EMBODYING ALL THAT IS VALUABLE IN THE WORKS OF

ROBERTS, HARMER, BURDER, PAXTON, CHANDLER,

And the most celebrated Oriental travellers. Embracing also the subject of the Fulfilment of Prophecy, as exhibited by Keith and others; with descriptions of the present state of countries and places mentioned in the Sacred Writings.

ILLUSTRATED BY NUMEROUS LANDSCAPE ENGRAVINGS,

FROM SKETCHES TAKEN ON THE SPOT.

EDITED BY REV. GEORGE BUSH,

Prof. of Hebrew and Oriental Literature in the N. Y. City University.

THE ILLUSTRATED CONCORDANCE,

In one volume, royal 8vo.

A new, full, and complete Concordance; illustrated with monumental, traditional, and oriental engravings, founded on Butterworth's, with Cruden's definitions; forming, it is believed, on many accounts, a more valuable work than either Butterworth, Cruden, or any other similar book in the language.

LIPPINCOTT'S STANDARD EDITIONS OF

THE BOOK OF COMMON PRAYER;

IN SIX DIFFERENT SIZES.

ILLUSTRATED WITH A NUMBER OF STEEL PLATES AND ILLUMINATIONS.

COMPREHENDING THE MOST VARIED AND SPLENDID ASSORTMENT IN THE UNITED STATES.

LIPPINCOTT'S EDITIONS OF

THE HOLY BIBLE,

SIX DIFFERENT SIZES.

Printed in the best manner, with beautiful type, on the finest sized paper, and bound in the most splendid and substantial styles. Warranted to be correct, and equal to the best English editions, at a much lower price. To be had with or without plates; the publishers having supplied themselves with over fifty steel engravings, by the first artists.

Baxter's Comprehensive Bible,

Royal quarto, containing the various readings and marginal notes, disquisitions on the genuineness, authenticity, and inspiration of the Holy Scriptures; introductory and concluding remarks to each book; philological and explanatory notes; tables of contents, arranged in historical order; a chronological index, and various other matter; forming a suitable book for the study of clergymen, Sabbath-school teachers and students.

The Oxford Quarto Bible,

Without note or comment, universally admitted to be the most beautiful family Bible extant.

Crown Octavo Bible,

Printed with large clear type, making a most convenient Bible for family use.

Polyglot Bible.

The Sunday-School Teacher's Polyglot Bible, with Maps, &c.

The Oxford 18mo. Bible.

This is an extremely handsome and convenient Pew Bible.

Agate 32mo. Bible,

Printed with larger type than any other small pocket edition extant.

32mo. Diamond Pocket Bible,

The neatest, smallest, and cheapest edition of the Bible published.

CONSTANTLY ON HAND,

A large assortment of BIBLES, bound in the most splendid and costly styles, with gold and silver ornaments, suitable for presentation; ranging in price from $10 00 tc $100 00.

A liberal discount made to Booksellers and Agents by the Publishers.

ENCYCLOPÆDIA OF RELIGIOUS KNOWLEDGE;

OR, DICTIONARY OF THE BIBLE THEOLOGY, RELIGIOUS BIOGRAPHY ALL RELIGIONS, ECCLESIASTICAL HISTORY, AND MISSIONS.

In one volume, royal 8vo.

SPLENDID LIBRARY EDITIONS.

ILLUSTRATED STANDARD POETS.

ELEGANTLY PRINTED, ON FINE PAPER, AND UNIFORM IN SIZE AND STYLE.

The following Editions of Standard British Poets are illustrated with numerous Steel Engravings, and may be had in all varieties of binding.

BYRON'S WORKS.

COMPLETE, IN ONE VOLUME, OCTAVO.

INCLUDING ALL HIS SUPPRESSED AND ATTRIBUTED POEMS; WITH SIX BEAUTIFUL ENGRAVINGS.

THE POETICAL WORKS OF MRS. HEMANS.

COMPLETE, IN ONE VOLUME, OCTAVO; WITH SEVEN BEAUTIFUL ENGRAVINGS.

MILTON, YOUNG, GRAY, BEATTIE, AND COLLINS'S POETICAL WORKS.

COMPLETE IN ONE VOLUME, OCTAVO.

WITH SIX BEAUTIFUL ENGRAVINGS.

Cowper and Thomson's Prose and Poetical Works.

COMPLETE IN ONE VOLUME, OCTAVO.

Including two hundred and fifty Letters, and sundry Poems of Cowper, never before published in this country; and a new and interesting Memoir of Thomson, and upwards of twenty new Poems, printed for the first time, from his own Manuscripts, taken from a late Edition of the Aldine Poets, now being published in London.

WITH SEVEN BEAUTIFUL ENGRAVINGS.

THE POETICAL WORKS OF ROGERS, CAMPBELL, MONTGOMERY, LAMB, AND KIRKE WHITE.

COMPLETE IN ONE VOLUME, OCTAVO.

WITH SIX BEAUTIFUL ENGRAVINGS.

CRABBE, HEBER, AND POLLOK'S POETICAL WORKS.

COMPLETE IN ONE VOLUME, OCTAVO.

WITH SIX BEAUTIFUL ENGRAVINGS.

No Library can be considered complete without a copy of the above beautiful and cheap editions of the English Poets; and persons ordering all or any of them, will please say, LIPPINCOTT, GRAMBO & Co.'s illustrated edition.

A COMPLETE

Dictionary of Poetical Quotations:

COMPRISING THE MOST EXCELLENT AND APPROPRIATE PASSAGES IN THE OLD BRITISH POETS; WITH CHOICE AND COPIOUS SELECTIONS FROM THE BEST MODERN BRITISH AND AMERICAN POETS.

EDITED BY SARAH JOSEPHA HALE.

As nightingales do upon glow-worms feed,
So poets live upon the living light
Of Nature and of Beauty.

Bailey's Festus.

Beautifully illustrated with Engravings. In one super-royal octavo volume, in various bindings.

THE DIAMOND EDITION OF BYRON.

THE POETICAL WORKS OF LORD BYRON.

WITH A SKETCH OF HIS LIFE.

COMPLETE IN ONE NEAT DUODECIMO VOLUME, WITH STEEL PLATES.

THE POETICAL WORKS OF THOMAS MOORE,

COLLECTED BY HIMSELF.

COMPLETE IN ONE VOLUME.

This work is published uniform with Byron, from the last London edition, and is the most complete printed in the country.

THE DIAMOND EDITION OF SHAKSPEARE.

(COMPLETE IN ONE VOLUME.)

INCLUDING A COPIOUS GLOSSARY.

UNIFORM WITH BYRON AND MOORE.

THE FOREGOING WORKS CAN BE HAD IN SEVERAL VARIETIES OF BINDING.

SCHOOLCRAFT'S GREAT NATIONAL WORK ON THE INDIAN TRIBES OF THE UNITED STATES.

WITH BEAUTIFUL AND ACCURATE COLOURED ILLUSTRATIONS.

HISTORICAL AND STATISTICAL INFORMATION

RESPECTING THE

HISTORY, CONDITION AND PROSPECTS

OF THE

Indian Tribes of the United States.

COLLECTED AND PREPARED UNDER THE DIRECTION OF THE BUREAU OF INDIAN AFFAIRS, PER ACT OF MARCH 3, 1847.

BY HENRY R. SCHOOLCRAFT, LL. D.

ILLUSTRATED BY S. EASTMAN, CAPT. U. S. A.

PUBLISHED BY AUTHORITY OF CONGRESS.

The Traveller's and Tourist's Guide

THROUGH THE UNITED STATES OF AMERICA, CANADA, ETC.

CONTAINING THE ROUTES OF TRAVEL BY STEAMBOAT, STAGE, AND CANAL; TOGETHER WITH DESCRIPTIONS OF, AND ROUTES TO, THE PRINCIPAL PLACES OF FASHIONABLE AND HEALTHFUL RESORT; WITH OTHER VALUABLE INFORMATION.

ACCOMPANIED BY

AN ENTIRELY NEW AND AUTHENTIC MAP OF THE UNITED STATES,

INCLUDING CALIFORNIA, OREGON, &c., AND A MAP OF THE ISLAND OF CUBA.

BY W. WILLIAMS.

THE AMERICAN GARDENER'S CALENDAR,

ADAPTED TO THE CLIMATE AND SEASONS OF THE UNITED STATES.

Containing a complete account of all the work necessary to be done in the Kitchen Garden, Fruit Garden, Orchard, Vineyard, Nursery, Pleasure-Ground, Flower Garden, Green-house, Hot-house, and Forcing Frames, for every month in the year; with ample Practical Directions for performing the same

BY BERNARD M'MAHON.

Tenth Edition, greatly improved. In one volume, octavo.

MASON'S FARRIER AND STUD BOOK—NEW EDITION.

Price, $1.

THE GENTLEMAN'S NEW POCKET FARRIER:

COMPRISING A GENERAL DESCRIPTION OF THE NOBLE AND USEFUL ANIMAL,

THE HORSE;

WITH MODES OF MANAGEMENT IN ALL CASES, AND TREATMENT IN DISEASE.

BY RICHARD MASON, M.D.,

Formerly of Surry County, Virginia.

TO WHICH IS ADDED,

A PRIZE ESSAY ON MULES; AND AN APPENDIX,

Containing Recipes for Diseaes of Horses, Oxen, Cows, Calves, Sheep, Dogs, Swine, &c., &c.; with Annals of the Turf, American Stud-Book, Rules for Training, Racing, &c., &c.

WITH A SUPPLEMENT,

BY J. S. SKINNER,

Editor of the Farmers' Library, New York, &c., &c.

MASON'S FARRIER—FARMERS' EDITION.

Price, 62 Cents.

THE PRACTICAL FARRIER, FOR FARMERS:

COMPRISING A GENERAL DESCRIPTION OF THE NOBLE AND USEFUL ANIMAL,

THE HORSE;

WITH MODES OF MANAGEMENT IN ALL CASES, AND TREATMENT IN DISEASE.

TO WHICH IS ADDED,

A PRIZE ESSAY ON MULES; AND AN APPENDIX,

Containing Recipes for Diseases of Horses, Oxen, Cows, Calves, Sheep, Dogs, Swine, &c.

BY RICHARD MASON, M.D.

FORMERLY OF SURRY COUNTY, VIRGINIA.

In one volume, 12mo.; bound in cloth, gilt.

HINDS'S FARRIERY AND STUD-BOOK—NEW EDITION.

FARRIERY,

TAUGHT ON A NEW AND EASY PLAN:

BEING A

Treatise on the Diseases and Accidents of the Horse;

With Instructions to the Shoeing Smith, Farrier, and Groom; preceded by a Popular description of the Animal Functions in Health, and how these are to be restored when disordered.

BY JOHN HINDS, VETERINARY SURGEON.

With considerable Additions and Improvements, particularly adapted to this country,

BY THOMAS M. SMITH,

Veterinary Surgeon, and Member of the London Veterinary Medical Society.

WITH A SUPPLEMENT, BY J. S. SKINNER.

TO CARPENTERS AND MECHANICS.

JUST PUBLISHED.

A NEW AND IMPROVED EDITION OF

THE CARPENTER'S NEW GUIDE,

BEING A COMPLETE BOOK OF LINES FOR

CARPENTRY AND JOINERY;

Treating fully on Practical Geometry, Saffit's Brick and Plaster Groins, Niches of every description, Sky-lights, Lines for Roofs and Domes; with a great variety of Designs for Roofs, Trussed Girders, Floors, Domes, Bridges, &c., Angle Bars for Shop Fronts, &c., and Raking Mouldings.

ALSO,

Additional Plans for various Stair-Cases, with the Lines for producing the Face and Falling Moulds, never before published, and greatly superior to those given in a former edition of this work.

BY WM. JOHNSON, ARCHITECT,

OF PHILADELPHIA.

The whole founded on true Geometrical Principles; the Theory and Practice well explained and fully exemplified, on eighty-three Copper-Plates, including some Observations and Calculations on the Strength of Timber.

BY PETER NICHOLSON,

Author of "The Carpenter and Joiner's Assistant," "The Student's Instructor to the Five Orders," &c.

Thirteenth Edition. One volume. 4to.. well bound.

SAY'S POLITICAL ECONOMY.

A TREATISE ON POLITICAL ECONOMY;

Or, The Production, Distribution and Consumption of Wealth.

BY JEAN BAPTISTE SAY.

FIFTH AMERICAN EDITION, WITH ADDITIONAL NOTES.

BY C. C. BIDDLE, Esq.

In one volume, octavo.

A BEAUTIFUL AND VALUABLE PRESENTATION BOOK.

THE POET'S OFFERING.

EDITED BY MRS. HALE.

With a Portrait of the Editress, a Splendid Illuminated Title-Page, and Twelve Beautiful Engravings by Sartain. Bound in rich Turkey Morocco, and Extra Cloth, Gilt Edge.

A Dictionary of Select and Popular Quotations,

WHICH ARE IN DAILY USE.

TAKEN FROM THE LATIN, FRENCH, GREEK, SPANISH AND ITALIAN LANGUAGES.

Together with a copious Collection of Law Maxims and Law Terms, translated into English, with Illustrations, Historical and Idiomatic.

NEW AMERICAN EDITION, CORRECTED, WITH ADDITIONS.

In one volume, 12mo.

The City Merchant; or, The Mysterious Failure.

BY J. B. JONES,

Author of "Wild Western Scenes," "The Western Merchant," &c.

ILLUSTRATED WITH TEN ENGRAVINGS.

In one volume, 12mo.

LAURENCE STERNE'S WORKS,

WITH A LIFE OF THE AUTHOR:

WRITTEN BY HIMSELF.

WITH SEVEN BEAUTIFUL ILLUSTRATIONS, ENGRAVED BY GILBERT AND GIHON, FROM DESIGNS BY DARLEY.

One volume, octavo; cloth, gilt.

RUSCHENBERGER'S NATURAL HISTORY.

COMPLETE, WITH NEW GLOSSARY.

THE ELEMENTS OF NATURAL HISTORY,

EMBRACING ZOOLOGY, BOTANY, AND GEOLOGY:

FOR SCHOOLS, COLLEGES, AND FAMILIES.

BY W. S. W. RUSCHENBERGER, M.D.

IN TWO VOLUMES.

WITH NEARLY ONE THOUSAND ILLUSTRATIONS, AND A COPIOUS GLOSSARY.

Vol. I. contains *Vertebrate Animals*. Vol. II. contains *Intervertebrate Animals, Botany, and Geology.*

The Mexican War and its Heroes;

BEING

A COMPLETE HISTORY OF THE MEXICAN WAR,

EMBRACING ALL THE OPERATIONS UNDER GENERALS TAYLOR AND SCOTT.

WITH A BIOGRAPHY OF THE OFFICERS.

ALSO,

AN ACCOUNT OF THE CONQUEST OF CALIFORNIA AND NEW MEXICO,

Under Gen. Kearney, Cols. Doniphan and Fremont. Together with Numerous Anecdotes of the War, and personal adventures of the Officers. Illustrated with Accurate Portraits and other Beautiful Engravings.

In one volume, 12mo.

A Book for every Family.

THE DICTIONARY OF

Domestic Medicine and Household Surgery.

BY SPENCER THOMPSON, M.D., F.R.C.S.,

Of Edinburgh.

ILLUSTRATED WITH NUMEROUS CUTS.

EDITED AND ADAPTED TO THE WANTS OF THIS COUNTRY, BY A WELL-KNOWN PRACTITIONER OF PHILADELPHIA.

In one volume, demi-octavo.

NEW AND COMPLETE COOK-BOOK.

THE PRACTICAL COOK-BOOK,

CONTAINING UPWARDS OF

ONE THOUSAND RECEIPTS,

Consisting of Directions for Selecting, Preparing, and Cooking all kinds of Meats, Fish, Poultry, and Game; Soups, Broths, Vegetables, and Salads. Also, for making all kinds of Plain and Fancy Breads, Pastes, Puddings, Cakes, Creams, Ices, Jellies, Preserves, Marmalades, &c., &c., &c. Together with various Miscellaneous Recipes, and numerous Preparations for Invalids.

BY MRS. BLISS.

In one volume, 12mo.

THE YOUNG DOMINICAN;
OR, THE MYSTERIES OF THE INQUISITION,

AND OTHER SECRET SOCIETIES OF SPAIN.

BY M. V. DE FEREAL.

WITH HISTORICAL NOTES, BY M. MANUEL DE CUENDIAS.

TRANSLATED FROM THE FRENCH.

ILLUSTRATED WITH TWENTY SPLENDID ENGRAVINGS BY FRENCH ARTISTS.

One volume, octavo.

TALES OF THE SOUTHERN BORDER.

BY C. W. WEBBER.

ONE VOLUME OCTAVO, HANDSOMELY ILLUSTRATED.

Price $1 50.

Gems from the Sacred Mine;

OR, HOLY THOUGHTS UPON SACRED SUBJECTS.

BY CLERGYMEN OF THE EPISCOPAL CHURCH.

EDITED BY THOMAS WYATT, A. M.

In one volume, 12mo.

WITH SEVEN BEAUTIFUL STEEL ENGRAVINGS.

The Daughter's Own Book:
OR, PRACTICAL HINTS FROM A FATHER TO HIS DAUGHTER.
In one volume, 18mo.

THE LIFE AND OPINIONS OF TRISTRAM SHANDY, GENTLEMAN.
COMPRISING THE HUMOROUS ADVENTURES OF
UNCLE TOBY AND CORPORAL TRIM.
BY L. STERNE.

Beautifully Illustrated by Darley. Stitched.

A SENTIMENTAL JOURNEY.
BY L. STERNE.

ILLUSTRATED AS ABOVE BY DARLEY. STITCHED.

The beauties of this author are so well known, and his errors in style and expression so few and far between, that one reads with renewed delight his delicate turns, &c.

ROBOTHAM'S POCKET FRENCH DICTIONARY.
CAREFULLY REVISED,

AND THE PRONUNCIATION OF ALL THE DIFFICULT WORDS ADDED.

THE YOUNG CHORISTER;
A Collection of New and Beautiful Tunes, adapted to the use of Sabbath-Schools, from some of the most distinguished composers, together with many of the author's compositions.

EDITED BY MINARD W. WILSON.

HOME GARNER:
OR, THE INTELLECTUAL AND MORAL STOREHOUSE:
GATHERED FOR THE FAMILY CIRCLE,

FROM THE RICH EXPERIENCE OF MANY FAITHFUL REAPERS.

BY MRS. MARY G. CLARKE.

In one volume. Illustrated with numerous engravings. $1 50.

APPLES OF GOLD.

(From Fenelon.)

32mo., CLOTH, GILT. PRICE 13 CENTS.

LIFE OF PAUL JONES.

In one volume, 12mo.

WITH ONE HUNDRED ILLUSTRATIONS.

BY JAMES HAMILTON.

THE LIFE OF GENERAL JACKSON,

WITH A LIKENESS OF THE OLD HERO.

In one volume, 18mo.

LIFE OF GENERAL ZACHARY TAYLOR,

COMPRISING A NARRATIVE OF EVENTS CONNECTED WITH HIS PROFESSIONAL CAREER, AND AUTHENTIC INCIDENTS OF HIS EARLY YEARS.

BY J. REESE FRY AND R. T. CONRAD.

With an original and accurate Portrait, and Eleven Elegant Illustrations, by Darley.

In one handsome 12mo volume.

GENERAL TAYLOR AND HIS STAFF:

Comprising Memoirs of Generals Taylor, Worth, Wool, and Butler; Colonels May, Cross, Clay, Hardin, Yell, Hays, and other distinguished Officers attached to General Taylor's Army.

INTERSPERSED WITH

NUMEROUS ANECDOTES OF THE MEXICAN WAR,

AND PERSONAL ADVENTURES OF THE OFFICERS.

Compiled from Public Documents and Private Correspondence.

WITH ACCURATE PORTRAITS AND OTHER BEAUTIFUL ILLUSTRATIONS.

In one volume, 12mo.

MECHANICS

FOR THE MILLWRIGHT, ENGINEER, AND MACHINIST, CIVIL ENGINEER AND ARCHITECT:

CONTAINING

THE PRINCIPLES OF MECHANICS APPLIED TO MACHINERY

Of American Models, Steam-Engines, Water-Works, Navigation, Bridge-building, &c., &c.

BY FREDERICK OVERMAN,

AUTHOR OF "THE MANUFACTURE OF IRON," AND OTHER SCIENTIFIC TREATISES.

Illustrated by 150 Engravings.

In one large 12mo. volume.

CALIFORNIA AND OREGON:

Or, Sights in the Gold Region, and Scenes by the Way.

BY THEODORE T. JOHNSON.

WITH A MAP AND ILLUSTRATIONS.

THIRD EDITION, WITH AN APPENDIX,

Containing Full Instructions to Emigrants by the Overland Route to Oregon.

BY HON. SAMUEL R. THURSTON,

Delegate to Congress from that Territory.

WILD WESTERN SCENES:

A NARRATIVE OF ADVENTURES IN THE WESTERN WILDERNESS.

Wherein the Exploits of Daniel Boone, the Great American Pioneer, are particularly described. Also, Minute Accounts of Bear, Deer, and Buffalo Hunts; Desperate Conflicts with the Savages; Fishing and Fowling Adventures; Encounters with Serpents, &c., &c.

BY LUKE SHORTFIELD,

Author of "The Western Merchant."

WITH SIXTEEN BEAUTIFUL ILLUSTRATIONS.

In one volume, 12mo.

POEMS OF THE PLEASURES:

CONSISTING OF

THE PLEASURES OF IMAGINATION, by Akenside; THE PLEASURES OF MEMORY, by Samuel Rogers; THE PLEASURES OF HOPE, by Campbell; and THE PLEASURES OF FRIENDSHIP, by M'Henry.

WITH A MEMOIR OF EACH AUTHOR,

Prepared expressly for this Work.

One volume, 18mo.

Nelly Bracken.

A TALE OF FORTY YEARS AGO.

BY ANNIE CHAMBERS BRADFORD.

In one volume, 12mo.

ARTHUR'S LIBRARY FOR THE HOUSEHOLD.

In Twelve handsome 18mo. volumes, bound in scarlet cloth, and each work complete in itself.

1. WOMEN'S TRIALS; OR, TALES AND SKETCHES FROM THE LIFE AROUND US.
2. MARRIED LIFE; ITS SHADOWS AND SUNSHINE.
3. THE TWO WIVES; OR, LOST AND WON.
4. THE WAYS OF PROVIDENCE; OR, "HE DOETH ALL THINGS WELL."
5. HOME SCENES.
6. STORIES FOR YOUNG HOUSEKEEPERS.
7. LESSONS IN LIFE, FOR ALL WHO WILL READ THEM.
8. SEED-TIME AND HARVEST; OR, WHATSOEVER A MAN SOWETH THAT SHALL HE ALSO REAP.
9. STORIES FOR PARENTS.
10. OFF-HAND SKETCHES, A LITTLE DASHED WITH HUMOR.
11. WORDS FOR THE WISE.
12. THE TRIED AND THE TEMPTED.

The above Series are sold together or separate, as each work is complete in itself. No family should be without a copy of this interesting and instructive Series. Price Thirty-seven and a Half Cents per Volume.

BALDWIN'S PRONOUNCING GAZETTEER.

A PRONOUNCING GAZETTEER:

Containing Topographical, Statistical, and other Information, of the more important Places in the known World, from the most recent and authentic Sources.

BY THOMAS BALDWIN,

Assisted by several other Gentlemen.

To which is added an APPENDIX, containing more than TEN THOUSAND ADDITIONAL NAMES, chiefly of the small Towns and Villages, &c., of the United States and of Mexico.

NINTH EDITION, WITH A SUPPLEMENT,

Giving the Pronunciation of near two thousand names, besides those pronounced in the Original Work: Forming in itself a Complete Vocabulary of Geographical Pronunciation.

ONE VOLUME 12MO.—PRICE, $1 50.

FIELD'S SCRAP BOOK.—NEW EDITION.

Literary and Miscellaneous Scrap Book.

Consisting of Tales and Anecdotes—Biographical, Historical, Moral, Religious, and Sentimental Pieces, in Prose and Poetry.

COMPILED BY WM. FIELDS.

SECOND EDITION, REVISED AND IMPROVED.

In one handsome 8vo. Volume. Price, $2 00.

PEPYS' DIARY.

DIARY AND CORRESPONDENCE

OF

SAMUEL PEPYS, F.R.S.

SECRETARY TO THE ADMIRALTY IN THE REIGNS OF CHARLES II. AND JAMES II.

FROM THE ORIGINAL SHORT-HAND MS. IN THE PEPYSIAN LIBRARY, WITH A LIFE AND NOTES.

BY RICHARD LORD BRAYBROOKE.

First American, from the Fifth London Edition.

In four volumes. Price, $5

THE CONFESSIONS OF A HOUSEKEEPER.

BY MRS. JOHN SMITH.

WITH THIRTEEN HUMOROUS ILLUSTRATIONS.

One Volume 12mo. Price 50 Cents.

THE HUMAN BODY AND ITS CONNEXION WITH MAN.

ILLUSTRATED BY THE PRINCIPAL ORGANS.

BY JAMES JOHN GARTH WILKINSON.

Member of the Royal College of Surgeons of England.

IN ONE VOLUME 12MO.—PRICE, $1 25.

BRADDOCK'S DEFEAT.

The History of an Expedition

AGAINST FORT DU QUESNE, IN 1775,

UNDER MAJOR-GENERAL EDWARD BRADDOCK.

Edited from the original MSS.,

BY WINTHROP SARGENT, M.A.

MEMBER OF THE HISTORICAL SOCIETY OF PENNSYLVANIA.

In one volume, octavo. $3.

Rifle and Light Infantry Tactics,

FOR THE EXERCISE AND MANŒUVRES OF TROOPS.

PREPARED UNDER THE DIRECTION OF THE WAR DEPARTMENT,

BY BREVET LIEUT. COL. W. J. HARDEE, U. S. ARMY.

In two volumes. $1 50.

CAVALRY TACTICS.

PRINTED BY ORDER OF THE WAR DEPARTMENT.

In two volumes. $2 50.

ELLET ON THE OHIO AND MISSISSIPPI RIVERS.

With Twelve Illustrations. One volume octavo. Price $3.

THIRTY YEARS WITH THE INDIAN TRIBES.

PERSONAL MEMOIRS OF A

Residence of Thirty Years with the Indian Tribes

ON THE AMERICAN FRONTIERS:

With brief Notices of passing Events, Facts, and Opinions.

A. D. 1812 TO A. D. 1842.

BY HENRY R. SCHOOLCRAFT.

One large 8vo. Volume. Price $3 00.

THE SCALP HUNTERS;

OR,

ROMANTIC ADVENTURES IN NORTHERN MEXICO.

BY CAPTAIN MAYNE REID,

Author of he "Rifle Rangers."

COMPLETE IN ONE VOLUME. PRICE FIFTY CENTS.

BOARDMAN'S BIBLE IN THE FAMILY.

The Bible in the Family:

OR, HINTS ON DOMESTIC HAPPINESS.

BY H. A. BOARDMAN.

PASTOR OF THE TENTH PRESBYTERIAN CHURCH, PHILADELPHIA.

One Volume 12mo.—Price One Dollar.

THE REGICIDE'S DAUGHTER:

A Tale of two Worlds.

BY W. H. CARPENTER,

AUTHOR OF "CLAIBORNE THE REBEL," "JOHN THE BOLD," &C., &C.

One Volume 18mo. Price Thirty-seven and a Half Cents.

SCHOOLCRAFTS GREAT NATIONAL WORK

ON THE

Indian Tribes of the United States.

PART SECOND—QUARTO.

WITH EIGHTY BEAUTIFUL ILLUSTRATIONS ON STEEL,

Engraved in the first style of the art, from Drawings by Capt. Eastman, U.S.A.

PRICE, FIFTEEN DOLLARS.

COCKBURN'S LIFE OF LORD JEFFREY.

LIFE OF LORD JEFFREY,

WITH

A SELECTION FROM HIS CORRESPONDENCE,

BY LORD COCKBURN,

One of the Judges of the Court of Sessions in Scotland.

2 vols. 12mo. Price, $2 50.

ROMANCE OF NATURAL HISTORY;

OR, WILD SCENES AND WILD HUNTERS.

WITH NUMEROUS ILLUSTRATIONS, ONE VOLUME OCTAVO, CLOTH.

BY C. W. WEBBER,

Author of "Old Hicks the Guide," "Shot in the Eye," &c.

PRICE, TWO DOLLARS.

THE LIFE OF WILLIAM PENN,

WITH

SELECTIONS FROM HIS CORRESPONDENCE AND AUTOBIOGRAPHY.

BY SAMUEL M. JANNEY.

Second Edition, Revised. Price, Two Dollars.

LIPPINCOTT'S CABINET HISTORIES OF THE STATES,

BY. T. S. ARTHUR and WM. H. CARPENTER.

FIRST SERIES OF TWELVE VOLUMES ALREADY COMPLETE,

COMPRISING THE HISTORY OF

Vermont, Massachusetts, Connecticut, N. York, N. Jersey, Pennsylvania, Virginia, Georgia, Tennessee, Kentucky, Ohio, Illinois.

Each History complete in one 12mo vol. of from 230 to 350 pages.

EXTRACTS FROM NOTICES OF THE PRESS.

"For School Libraries, and indeed for all Libraries, the Series will be found of great value."—*Buffalo Daily Courier.*

"They are eminently adapted both to interest and instruct, and should have a place in the Family Library of every American."—*New York Courier and Enquirer.*

"They contain the very pith and marrow of the record from the earliest periods down to the present time."—*Albany Express.*

"As a work for the young we know of none more suitable to put into their hands."—*Detroit Daily Advertiser.*

"They should be read by all who would know the annals of our country, and the wild legends on which our future epics and histories are to be built."—*Louisiana Courier.*

"Thousands of persons, old as well as young, will be tempted to read such volumes as these, and thus get a general knowledge of the history of the several States."—*Boston Traveller.*

"The value of such a Series cannot be too highly estimated."—*American Courier.*

"We predict great popularity for the Series."—*Philadelphia Evening Bulletin.*

"This will be of great practical value in extending a history of the individual States."—*Boston Journal.*

Price per volume, 42 cents.

New Themes for the Protestant Clergy;

CREEDS WITHOUT CHARITY, THEOLOGY WITHOUT HUMANITY, AND PROTESTANTISM WITHOUT CHRISTIANITY:

With Notes by the Editor on the Literature of Charity, Population, Pauperism, Political Economy, and Protestantism.

PRICE, ONE DOLLAR.

SIMPSON'S MILITARY JOURNAL.

JOURNAL OF A MILITARY RECONNOISSANCE FROM SANTA FE, NEW MEXICO, TO THE NAVAJO COUNTRY,

BY JAMES H. SIMPSON, A. M.,

FIRST LIEUTENANT CORPS OF TOPOGRAPHICAL ENGINEERS.

WITH 75 COLOURED ILLUSTRATIONS.

One volume, octavo. Price, Three Dollars.

In Press,

A NEW AND COMPLETE

GAZETTEER OF THE UNITED STATES.

It will furnish the fullest and most recent information respecting the Geography Statistics, and present state of improvement, of every part of this great Republic, particularly of

TEXAS, CALIFORNIA, OREGON, NEW MEXICO,

&c. The work will be issued as soon as the complete official returns of the present Census are received.

THE AMERICAN HANDBOOK OF ORNAMENTAL TREES.

BY THOMAS MEHAN, GARDENER.

In one volume, 18mo. Price, Seventy-five cents.

THE ADVENTURES OF HAJJI BABA,

IN TURKEY, PERSIA AND RUSSIA. 75 cents.

History of the Mormons

OF UTAH,

THEIR DOMESTIC POLITY AND THEOLOGY,

BY J. W. GUNNISON,

U. S. CORPS TOPOGRAPHICAL ENGINEERS.

WITH ILLUSTRATIONS, IN ONE VOLUME DEMI-OCTAVO.

REPORT OF A GEOLOGICAL SURVEY OF WISCONSIN, IOWA, AND MINNESOTA,

AND INCIDENTALLY OF A PORTION OF NEBRASKA TERRITORY,

MADE UNDER INSTRUCTIONS FROM THE U. S. TREASURY DEPART'M'T

BY DAVID DALE OWEN,

United States' Geologist.

WITH OVER 150 ILLUSTRATIONS ON STEEL AND WOOD.

TWO VOLUMES, QUARTO. PRICE $10 00.

MERCHANTS' MEMORANDUM BOOK,

WITH LISTS OF ALL GOODS PURCHASED BY COUNTRY MERCHANTS, &c.

One volume, 18mo., Leather cover. Price, 50 cents.

FROST'S JUVENILE SERIES.

TWELVE VOLUMES, 16mo., WITH FIVE HUNDRED ENGRAVINGS.

WALTER O'NEILL, OR THE PLEASURE OF DOING GOOD. 25 Engravings.
JUNKER SCHOTT, and other Stories. 6 Engravings.
THE LADY OF THE LURLEI, and other Stories. 12 Engravings.
ELLEN'S BIRTHDAY, and other Stories. 20 Engravings.
HERMAN, and other Stories. 9 Engravings.
KING TREGEWALL'S DAUGHTER, and other Stories. 16 Engr's.
THE DROWNED BOY, and other Stories. 6 Engravings.
THE PICTORIAL RHYME-BOOK. 122 Engravings.
THE PICTORIAL NURSERY BOOK. 117 Engravings.
THE GOOD CHILD'S REWARD. 115 Engravings.
ALPHABET OF QUADRUPEDS. 26 Engravings.
ALPHABET OF BIRDS. 26 Engravings.

PRICE, TWENTY-FIVE CENTS EACH.

The above popular and attractive series of New Juveniles for the Young, are sold together or separately.

Lights and Shadows of English Life.

BY THE

AUTHORESS OF "CLARA CAMERON: OR, THE BELLE OF THE SEASON."

In two volumes, duodecimo. $1 50.

STANSBURY'S
EXPEDITION TO THE GREAT SALT LAKE.

AN EXPLORATION
OF THE VALLEY OF THE GREAT SALT LAKE
OF UTAH,

CONTAINING ITS GEOGRAPHY, NATURAL HISTORY, MINERALOGICAL RESOURCES, ANALYSIS OF ITS WATERS, AND AN AUTHENTIC ACCOUNT OF

THE MORMON SETTLEMENT.

Also, A Reconnoissance of a New Route through the Rocky Mountains with Seventy Beautiful Illustrations, from Drawings taken on the spot, and two large and accurate Maps of that region.

BY HOWARD STANSBURY,

Captain Topographical Engineers. 2 vols. royal octavo. Price $5 00.

GRIMSHAW'S
Ladies' Lexicon and Parlour Companion:

CONTAINING

NEARLY EVERY WORD IN THE ENGLISH LANGUAGE,

AND EXHIBITING THE PLURALS OF NOUNS AND THE PARTICIPLES OF VERBS.

BY WILLIAM GRIMSHAW, ESQ.

One volume, 18mo. Price 50 cts.

THE COLUMBIAN ORATOR,

CONTAINING

A VARIETY OF ORIGINAL AND SELECTED PIECES.

TOGETHER WITH

RULES CALCULATED TO IMPROVE YOUTH AND OTHERS IN THE ORNAMENTAL AND USEFUL ART OF ELOQUENCE.

BY CALEB BINGHAM, A. M.,

Author of "The American Preceptor."

A NEW AND REVISED EDITION.

One vol. 12mo. Price 50 cents.

A POPULAR NOVEL.

LYNDE WEISS, AN AUTOBIOGRAPHY.

BY GEO. H. THROOP,

Author of "Nag's Head," "Bertie," &c. &c.

PRICE, PAPER, FIFTY CENTS. CLOTH, SEVENTY-FIVE CENTS.

PERSONAL MEMOIRS of DANIEL WEBSTER.

OCTAVO, STITCHED. PRICE 15 CENTS.

HEMANS' POETICAL WORKS.

COMPLETE IN ONE VOLUME, 12MO.

PRICE, CLOTH, 75 CENTS. EXTRA GILT EDGES, $1 25.

THE PHILADELPHIA HOUSEWIFE,
OR, FAMILY RECEIPT-BOOK.
BY AUNT MARY.
IN ONE VOLUME, 12MO. 75 cents.

CLINICAL LECTURES ON SURGERY.
BY M. NÉLATON.
FROM NOTES TAKEN BY WALTER F. ATLEE, M.D.

The U. S. Naval Astronomical Expedition
TO THE SOUTHERN HEMISPHERE,
DURING THE YEARS 1849, 1850, 1851, 1852,
UNDER LIEUTENANT J. M. GILLIS.

CHILE:
Its Geography, Climate, Earthquakes, Government, Social Condition, Mineral and Agricultural Resources, Commerce, etc.
BY LIEUT. J. M. GILLIS.
IN TWO VOLUMES, QUARTO.
Price, $10.

TEN NIGHTS IN A BAR-ROOM,
AND WHAT I SAW THERE.
BY T. S. ARTHUR.
IN ONE VOLUME, 12MO. 75 cents.

THE TWO ROADS,
OR, THE RIGHT AND THE WRONG.
BY JAMES KNORR.
IN ONE VOLUME, 12MO. $1.

MIRANDA ELLIOT,
OR,
THE VOICE OF THE SPIRIT.
In one volume, 12mo. $1.

A PRACTICAL TREATISE ON BUSINESS;

OR, HOW TO GET, SAVE, SPEND, GIVE, LEND, AND BEQUEATH MONEY

WITH AN INQUIRY INTO THE CHANCES OF SUCCESS AND CAUSES OF FAILURE IN BUSINESS.

BY EDWIN T. FREEDLY.

Also, Prize Essays, Statistics, Miscellanies, and numerous private letters from successful and distinguished business men.

12mo., cloth. Price One Dollar.

The object of this treatise is fourfold. First, the elevation of the business character, and to define clearly the limits within which it is not only proper but obligatory to get money. Secondly, to lay down the principles which must be observed to insure success, and what must be avoided to escape failure. Thirdly, to give the mode of management in certain prominent pursuits adopted by the most successful, from which men in all kinds of business may derive profitable hints. Fourthly, to afford a work of solid interest to those who read without expectation of pecuniary benefit.

TRUTHS ILLUSTRATED by GREAT AUTHORS.

A DICTIONARY OF OVER FOUR THOUSAND AIDS TO REFLECTION —QUOTATIONS OF MAXIMS, METAPHORS, COUNSELS, CAUTIONS, APHORISMS, PROVERBS, &c. &c., IN PROSE AND VERSE;

COMPILED FROM SHAKSPEARE, AND OTHER GREAT WRITERS, FROM THE EARLIEST AGES TO THE PRESENT TIME.

A new edition, with American additions and revisions.

ONE VOLUME, CROWN OCTAVO, VARIOUS BINDINGS.

The Footpath and Highway;

OR,

WANDERINGS OF AN AMERICAN IN GT. BRITAIN,

IN 1851 AND '52.

BY BENJAMIN MORAN.

This volume embodies the observations of the author, made during eight months' wanderings, as a correspondent for American Journals; and as he travelled much on foot, differs essentially from those on the same countries, by other writers. The habits, manners, customs, and condition of the people have been carefully noted, and his views of them are given in clear, bold language. His remarks take a wide range, and as he visited every county in England but three, there will be much in the work of a novel and instructive character.

One vol. 12mo. Price $1 25.

www.ingramcontent.com/pod-product-compliance
Lightning Source LLC
LaVergne TN
LVHW010211110826
845151LV00004B/1056
9781425528454